Art & Activities for Kids

Art Fun!

NORTH LIGHT BOOKS

Cincinnati, Ohio

A Note About Safety

The activities in this book were developed for the enjoyment of kids. We've taken every precaution to ensure their safety and success. Please follow the directions, and note where an adult's help is required. In fact, feel free to work alongside your young artists as often as you can. They will appreciate help in reading and learning new techniques, and will love the chance to talk and show off their creations.

Art Fun! Copyright © 1997 by F+W Publications, Inc. Manufactured in China. All rights reserved. No part of this book may be reproduced in any form or by any electronic or mechanical means including information storage and retrieval systems without permission in writing from the publisher, except by a reviewer, who may quote brief passages in a review. Published by North Light Books, an imprint of F+W Publications, Inc., 4700 East Galbraith Road, Cincinnati, Ohio 45236. (800) 289-0963. First edition.

Other fine North Light Books are available from your local bookstore, art supply store or direct from the publisher.

10 09 08 07 06   12 11 10 9 8

Library of Congress Cataloging-in-Publication Data

Art fun! / Kim Solga, project editor.—1st ed.
    p.   cm.—(Art & activities for kids)
  Summary: Presents step-by-step instructions for creating a wide variety of art projects through painting, drawing, print-making, and sculpture.
  ISBN-13: 978-0-89134-833-7 (alk. paper)
  ISBN-10: 0-89134-833-6 (alk. paper)
  1. Art—Technique—Juvenile literature. [1. Art—Technique.] I. Solga, Kim. II. Series.
N7440.A78   1997
372.5′044—dc21
                          97-1934
                            CIP
                            AC

Edited by Julie Wesling Whaley
Design Direction by Clare Finney
Art Direction by Kristi Kane Cullen
Photography by Pamela Monfort
Very special thanks to Theresa Brockman, Eric Deller, Jessica Dolle, Anita Drake, Libby Fellerhoff, Chris Keefe, Alison Wenstrup, Suzanne Whitaker and Rachel Wolf.

F·W PUBLICATIONS, INC.

Table of Contents

(Table of Contents continued on page 4) ▶

Be a Good Artist

Work Habits

Get permission to set up an art workshop before you begin. Cover your workspace with newspapers or a vinyl tablecloth. Wear a smock or big, old T-shirt to protect your clothes.

Have a ruler handy so you can measure things. This symbol, ", means inches—12" means 12 inches; cm means centimeters.

Most of the supplies you'll need for each project can be found around the house. Keep a few paper plates and egg cartons to mix paint in. Plastic margarine tubs are great for rinse water. Save old squeeze bottles and sponges. Look for unused white cloth and scrap cloth, old magazines and newspapers.

Collect things you can use to make interesting sculptures: shells, hardware, cardboard tubes, little toys, and stuff like feathers and sequins. Collect things you think will make good prints: leaves, feathers, spools, coins, hardware, and little toys. Make sure they're clean.

Sweep up scraps and clean up splatters and spills as soon as they happen. Always finish by cleaning your workspace and all your tools. Wash brushes in warm water until the water runs clear, and store with bristles up. Treat all of your art supplies with respect.

Art Terms

Tempera paint. Also called poster paint, tempera paint is water-based paint that is opaque—you can't see through it. Buy it at an art or school supply store already mixed with water, or as a powder that you mix with water (with an adult's help).

Watercolor paint. This water-based paint is transparent—you can see through it when you paint with it. It comes in little trays of dry paint that you get wet with a paintbrush and water.

Acrylic paint. This is a water-based plastic paint that's thick and shiny. It comes in a tube or squeeze bottle. You mix it with water to paint, but it's permanent once it's dry.

Fabric paint. This is the best paint to use on cloth. Get an adult to help you use fabric paint, and follow the instructions on the label.

Permanent markers and **fabric crayons** are other things you can use to put color on cloth. *Always have an adult help you* use them correctly.

Water-based printing ink. This is a nontoxic printmaking ink that comes in a tube. It's smooth and very sticky, but it washes off with soap and water.

Paintbrushes. There are many kinds of brushes. You may want to buy several, from thin ones to fat ones—even wide house painting brushes. You'll need a sponge or "foam" brush from the hardware store for some of the projects.

The clock symbol means you must wait to let something dry before going on to the next step. It is very important not to rush ahead.

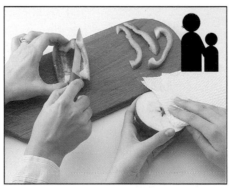

Follow the directions carefully for each project. When you see this symbol, have an adult help you.

Don't put art materials in your mouth. If you're working with a younger child, don't let him put art materials in his mouth, either.

Drawing paper. Any white paper, like writing paper or something heavier like construction paper, is good drawing paper.

Watercolor paper. This is a heavy, white or off-white paper with a bumpy surface. You can buy it wherever art supplies are sold.

Newsprint. This is gray paper that newspapers are printed on. This paper costs less than good, white paper like watercolor paper. Newsprint is available in rolls for big paintings (you can buy it at an art supply store, or ask any newspaper office for a "roll end").

Matboard. This is fancy cardboard that goes around a picture inside a frame. It comes in all colors at framing stores (ask for scraps) or art supply stores.

Tagboard. Also called poster board, tagboard is thinner than matboard. You can buy it wherever school supplies are sold.

Glue. Most of the projects in this book can be done with regular white glue. For projects where you use cloth, **fabric glue** works better because it's specially made for cloth. **Carpenter's glue** from a hardware store works best on heavy things like metal and wood.

Tape. **Masking tape** is fine for most of the projects in this book that call for tape. **Clear adhesive tape** works well for paper projects. **Duct tape** or **electrical tape** works best on plastic and metal.

Pencils. The "lead" in a pencil is made from graphite and clay. Some leads are soft and some are hard. Most artists like to use soft drawing pencils that make smooth, dark lines. Art pencils are marked with letters so you can tell how soft they are: "H" pencils are hard; "B" pencils are soft. The higher the number is, the harder or softer the lead is. For example, 6B is the very softest pencil. Common yellow pencils are #2, which really means 2B.

Charcoal pencils. These are fun to draw with, especially for making shadows because you can rub a charcoal mark with your fingertip to create different shades of gray. You can draw with charcoal sticks or fat pencils. Charcoal is made from specially burnt wood—it's *really* dark and soft. Be warned: They're more smudgy and messy that regular pencils!

Colored pencils. You can buy a whole set of colored pencils to make color drawings. They're better than crayons for making thin lines and for coloring in small spaces. They are cleaner than markers, and the colors are lighter and easier to blend.

Varnish. Varnish will add a shiny, waterproof finish to your work. *Always have an adult help you* brush on varnish or acrylic gloss medium after your paint is completely dry.

Acrylic gloss medium. This is a type of varnish that's nontoxic. It comes in a spray can or in liquid form that you apply with a brush. Even though it's not toxic, it's still best for adults to supervise the use of any spray product.

Brayer. This is a rubber roller used to spread a very thin layer of ink. You hold the brayer by its handle and roll it in ink poured in a shallow dish or pan. Then you roll it on the surface of a printing block or on an object you want to print with. See how to make your own brayer on page 91.

Ink pads. Ink pads are made for rubber stamps and they come in lots of great colors. Be sure to buy ink pads with nontoxic inks. Sometimes craft stores have fabric ink pads you can use on clothes.

India ink. There are lots of kinds and colors of India ink. You can buy a small bottle or a large jar of it at art supply stores. The best kind to use for tempera batik (page 184) is black, waterproof India ink.

Colored sand. You can find colored sand at craft and hobby stores, or you can get plain, fine sand and color it yourself. One way to color it is to buy colorful chalk and rub it on sandpaper to make powder. Then mix the powder with the sand.

Clay. A recipe for making sculpting dough is on page 156. You can also buy different kinds of clay at craft and art supply stores. Some dry in the air, others require baking, and others never get very hard so you can reuse them.

Plaster of Paris. This is a powder you can buy at a hardware store or art supply store. You mix it with water to make a white plaster that dries hard.

In Soft Stone Carving (page 144), you mix plaster of Paris with **vermiculite**, a type of soil you can buy at garden stores. The vermiculite will keep the plaster soft for a longer time so you can carve it easily. Vermiculite comes in different forms. The kind that looks ground up works better than the flaky kind, but either one is fine to use.

Part One: Paint!

A Note to Grown-Ups

Paint! features eleven unique painting projects plus numerous variations that will fire the imaginations of boys and girls aged six to eleven. By inviting kids to try new things, *Paint!* encourages individual creativity. Young artists will love "breaking the rules" of painting even while they're learning important principles of art. Rather than painting only with brushes, they'll be using craft sticks, cotton-tip swabs, fingers, marbles, and brushes they make themselves out of cotton and feathers—even balloons! They'll learn to make their own paints out of egg yolks and vegetable oil with ground chalk or powdered drink mix for pigments. Not limited to paper, they'll paint on cloth, foil, rocks, faces—even windows—all the while learning about blending colors, paint texture, translucency, proportion and much more.

Each project has a theme, stated at the very beginning, and some projects suggest follow-up activities related to that theme. Some projects result in beautiful finished works to display or give away; others emphasize experimentation and the simple fun of *doing* them. They're all kid-tested to ensure a high success rate and inspire confidence.

Getting the Most Out of the Projects

Each project is both fun to do and educational. While the projects provide clear step-by-step instructions and photographs, each is open-ended so kids may decide what *they* want to paint. Some of the projects are easy to do in a short amount of time. Others require more patience and even adult supervision.

The list of materials shown at the beginning of each activity is for the featured project only. Suggested alternatives may require different supplies. Feel free to substitute! For example, Pudding Paint recreates the thick texture of undiluted acrylic paint straight from the tube. If cooking up a batch of paint isn't for you, your child could do the activity with non-toxic acrylics, though this is a more expensive alternative. The projects offer flexibility to make it easy for you and your child to try as many activities as you wish.

Collecting Supplies

All of the projects can be done with household items or inexpensive, easy-to-find supplies. Here are some household items you'll want to make sure you have on hand: newspapers, paper plates, muffin tins or egg cartons (for holding and mixing different colors of paint), scrap paper, scrap cardboard, cotton swabs, squeeze bottle (from mustard or dish soap, for example), magazines (for photos and ideas), foil, plastic wrap, waxed paper, white glue, flour, salt, sugar, breakfast cereal, marbles, liquid laundry starch, white cloth and scrap cloth, sponges.

Crystal Colors

Color Blending

Have you ever found the windows covered with lacy frost on a cold, winter morning? Was it Jack Frost who painted the delicate designs, or simply water molecules freezing into crystal formations? This watercolor project captures the beautiful look of frost crystals in an explosion of color.

Materials needed:

Plastic wrap (about twice as big as the paper used)

Watercolors

Rinse water

Fat watercolor brushes

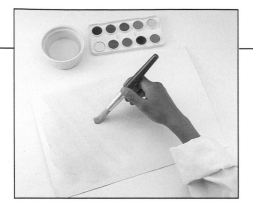

1 "Paint" clear water onto your paper. Then paint big patches of bright colors on the wet paper. Let the colors spread out and blend.

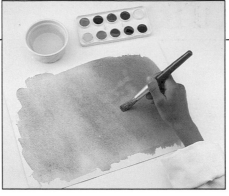

2 If you wish, drip and splatter on your color patches, but work quickly to cover your paper with pools of bright colors.

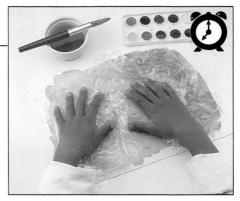

3 Crumple a big piece of plastic wrap and pat it gently down on top of your wet painting. Set it in a safe place to dry overnight.

White drawing paper or watercolor paper

Crystal Textures

When you pull the plastic off your dry painting, you'll be amazed at the texture left behind! You can get wonderful colors and patterns with colored ink, tempera paint and acrylics. Try pressing other materials onto wet paint. Experiment with as many different textures as you can!

Aluminum Foil

Waxed Paper

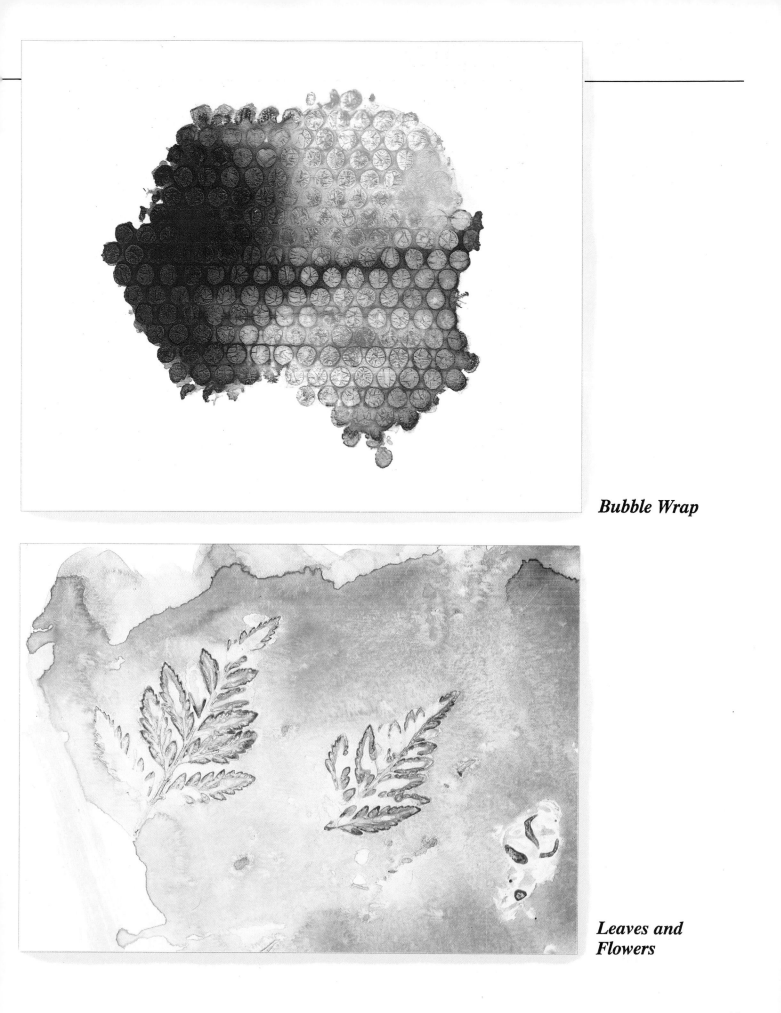

Bubble Wrap

Leaves and Flowers

Pudding Paint

Mastering Texture

Pudding Paint looks a lot like ketchup, mustard and mayonnaise, with some blueberry and chocolate pudding on the side. Not much of a snack, but you sure can have fun with this thick paint, cooked like pudding and spread on cardboard with craft sticks.

Pudding paint recipe: (Ask an adult to help you.) Mix 5 cups water, 2 cups white flour, ½ cup sugar, and 3 tablespoons salt. Pour into a saucepan and cook over medium heat until thick and bubbling (about 7 minutes). Cool well. This can be stored in the refrigerator in covered containers for several weeks.

Pudding paint mixture

Materials needed:

Craft sticks and a spoon

Tempera paint (powdered or liquid)

2 paper plates and 5 containers for mixing

1 Spoon cooled "pudding" into 5 containers and mix with ⅛- to ¼-cup powdered or liquid tempera paint to make 5 main colors.

2 Place spoonfuls of the main colors on one paper plate; use another plate to mix colors. Use craft sticks to paint on cardboard.

3 Pull up to get pointy peaks, or scrape a design into the paint. Make an abstract design, or paint a realistic picture.

Cardboard, tagboard or matboard (the heavier the better)

Recipes for Fun

Starchy Paint

Mix powdered tempera paint with liquid laundry starch.
Add just enough starch to make a thick, shiny paint. Work
with stiff brushes on cardboard.

Sawdust Paint

Add spoonfuls of sawdust or crushed breakfast cereal to any liquid paint for a grainy, bumpy texture.

Salt Paint

Stir regular table salt into liquid tempera for a thick, sandy paint. The mixture creates interesting textures as it dries.

Dots of Color

Exploring Pointillism

Painting a picture with dots instead of lines gives your work an extra special look. Here's a project that uses bright paint and cotton-tip swabs. Remember—paint only dots and dots and more dots!

Materials needed:

Yellow chalk

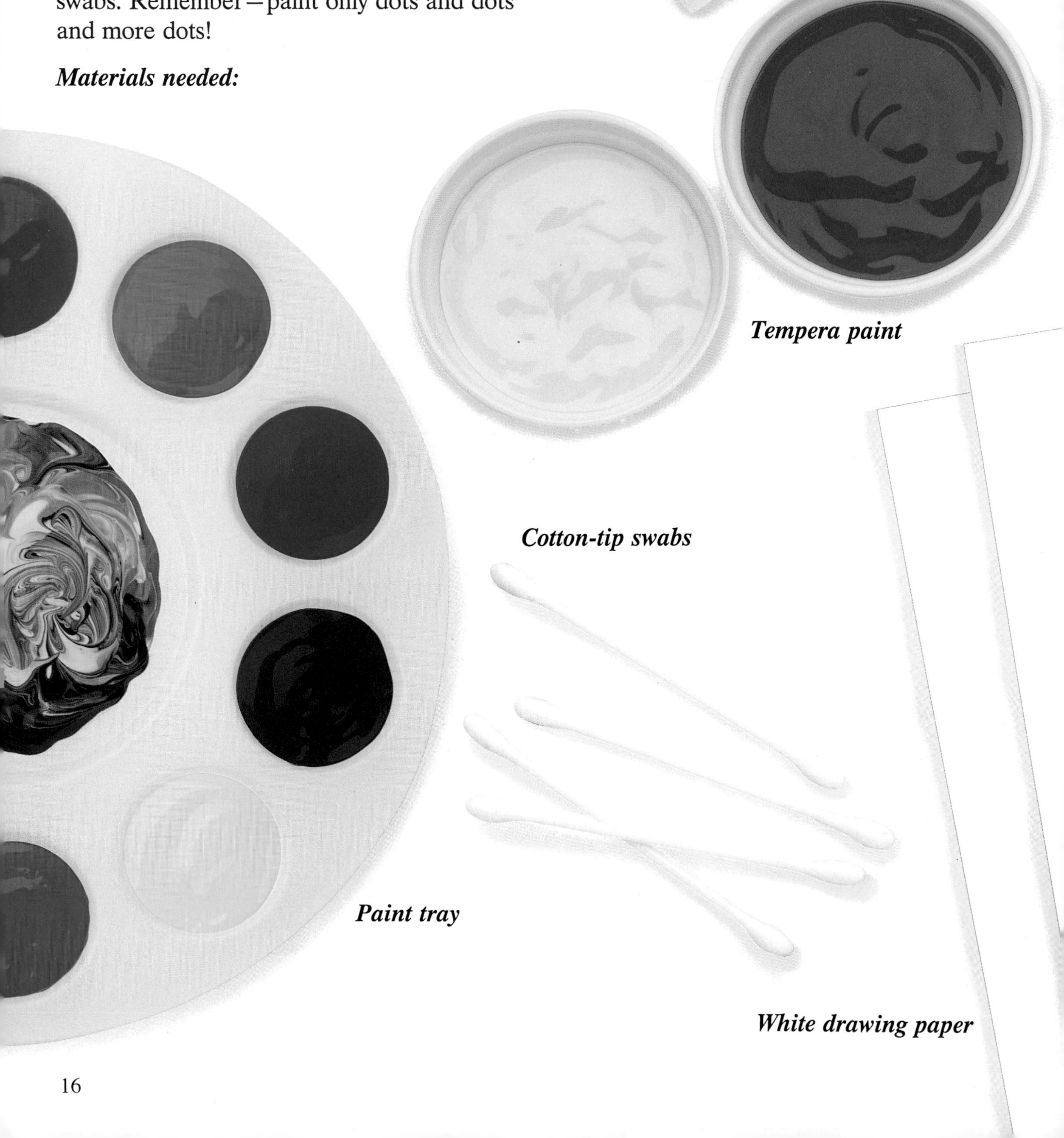

Tempera paint

Cotton-tip swabs

Paint tray

White drawing paper

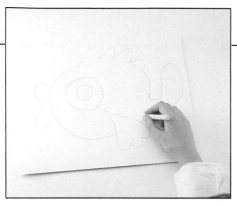

1 Sketch your picture lightly with yellow chalk. The faint lines will brush off easily when your painting is dry.

2 Outline the main shapes of your picture with cotton-tip swabs dipped in paint. Use a new swab for each color.

3 Fill in the shapes with more dots. For smaller dots, pull the cotton away and use just the cardboard stick.

Lots of Dots

Lots of subjects make great Dots of Color paintings! Even small objects you can trace look special when you fill in the familiar shapes with colored dots.

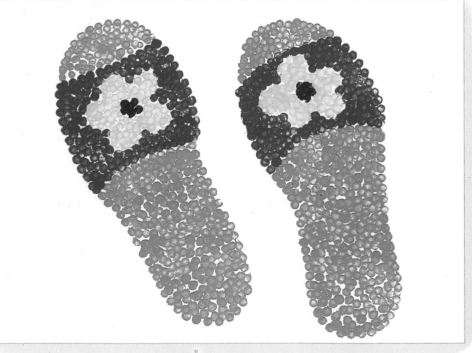

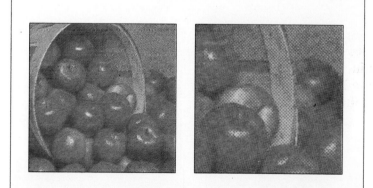

When you look at a picture printed in a magazine or newspaper, you see what appear to be solid colors. But they're actually dots of color! Look closely at the comics in the Sunday newspaper and you'll see it's true.

Stained Glass

Understanding Translucency

Have you ever seen stained glass windows in a church or old house? They're beautiful because they're *translucent*—they allow light to shine through. You can create a "stained glass" window in your home, with special paints you mix yourself.

Materials needed:

Paintbrushes

Pencil and a black marker

Tempera paint, water, liquid dish soap, and containers

Plastic squeeze bottle

1 Get permission to decorate a sunny window in your home. Cover the windowsill, floor, and the walls with newspaper.

2 Draw a stained glass design on paper first. Sketch a pattern or simple picture, leaving lots of open spaces for different colors.

3 Make your pencil lines dark or use a black marker. Tape your sketch to the outside of the window, with your design facing in.

Masking tape

**Drawing paper and
newspaper**

4 You'll need black paint as thick
as mayonnaise. Mix liquid
tempera paint with cornstarch or
flour if it needs thickening.

5 Spoon the thick black paint
into the squeeze bottle. It will be
easier to squeeze the paint out if the
bottle is full.

6 Squeeze black paint on the
inside of the window along the
outline of your design. Let it dry for
two hours.

Glass Art

Suncatcher

Make a suncatcher on a piece of acrylic (available at window and plate glass shops) or glass in an old picture frame. Follow these same directions. Then, when it's dry, attach a wire or small chain to the picture frame and hang it from a small nail in the frame of a sunny window.

7 Mix several colors of tempera paint with water and a bit of dish soap. The mixed paints should be runny like syrup.

8 When the black paint is all dry, use regular paintbrushes to paint your translucent colors into the spaces of your design.

9 Your stained glass painting can be cleaned off later with soap and water. You may have to scrape to get the black paint off.

Build a Better Brush

Art Has No Rules

What if you went on a camping trip to do some artwork, far away from any town, and you packed all your paints and paper but forgot your paintbrushes—what would you do? You'd have to invent your own! Here are some examples of handmade brushes. Try making them yourself, or create your own, and use them when you paint pictures.

The Balloon Brush
Tie four or five small balloons onto a stick with wire. Use them as they are or cut them into strips.

The Straw Brush
Make a stiff brush by tying together pieces of hay or straw—or pine needles—and attaching them to a stick.

The Housepet Brush
Gather a small handful of your dog's or cat's hair, bunch it together, and tie it onto a stick.

The Feather Brush
Paint a picture with a bunch of feathers held together with a twist of wire.

Bark Brushes
A piece of soft bark that is partially frayed apart makes a great brush.

Ready-Made Brushes
Some dry weeds make interesting brushes just the way they are. Try painting with a stalk of broccoli!

The Cotton Puff Brush
Secure a cotton ball to the end of a stick with a twist of wire.

Marble Rolling

Appreciating Abstract Design

Make beautiful rainbow-colored confetti paintings by rolling painted marbles (or beads or tennis balls) on paper taped in a box lid. It's so much fun, you won't want to stop!

Tempera paint

Marb

Materials needed:

Spoon and small dishes

Box lid

1 Pour paint into dishes and drop two or three marbles into each color. Lift them out and set them on paper taped in the box lid.

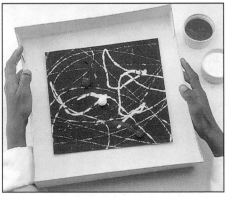

2 Tip the box lid so the marbles roll around. When the paint is used up, dunk the marbles back into the paint — add new colors.

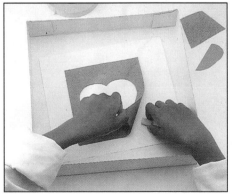

3 Try taping a smaller piece of paper in the middle of the larger one. When you lift it off, you'll see a white design left behind!

27

Face Painting

Painting Expressions

The artist becomes the art! Learn how to paint happy and sad, ferocious and curious—right on your own face. Painting expressions is an important part of making faces look realistic.

Materials needed:

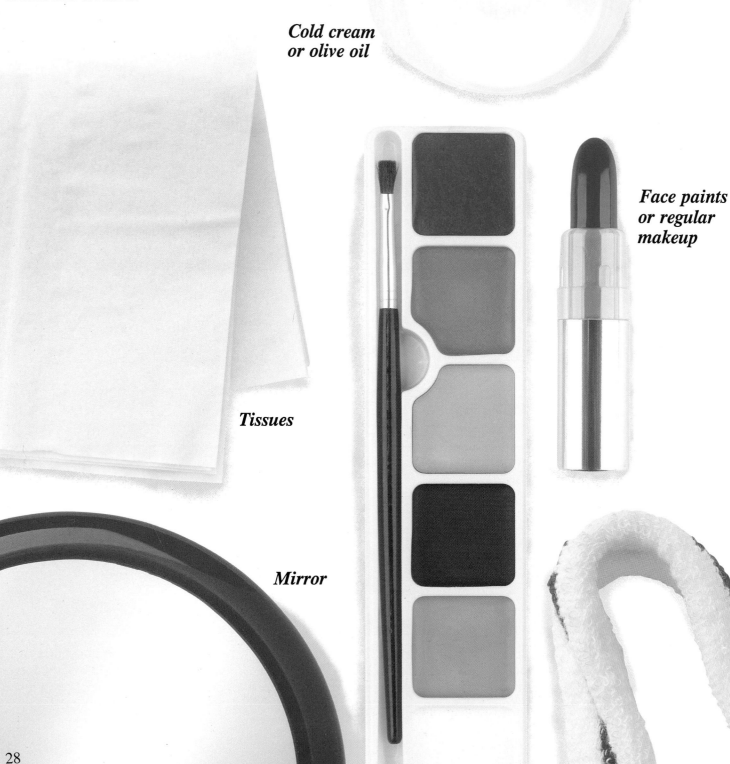

Towel

Cold cream or olive oil

Face paints or regular makeup

Tissues

Mirror

1 Hold your hair back with a headband and cover your clothes with a towel.

2 Rub cold cream or olive oil on your skin before using regular makeup.

3 Use your fingers or a small piece of sponge to spread paint on your skin.

4 Never get close to your eyes with oil, makeup or paint. Use a paintbrush to make fine lines.

Sponge pieces

Paintbrush

Headband

Makeup is easier to remove if you rub most of it off with cold cream or olive oil and tissues first, then wash with warm water and soap.

People Faces

Professional clowns begin with white and then add darker colors one by one. You should paint your face this way, too. Be careful not to smear colors together.

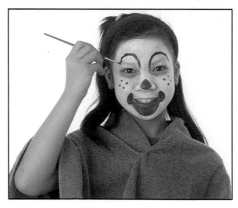

Happy Clown

Sad "Hobo" Clown

1 Paint your face white. Make a bright red smile and a red nose.

2 Add red freckles. Use black to make high, half-moon eyebrows and little sparkle lines by your eyes.

3 Paint a gray patch around your mouth. Paint a red nose and a big red frown. Darken your eyebrows and add a teardrop.

Monster

Zany Face

4 Make a scar! Spread a thin line of *nontoxic* white glue on one cheek. Pinch your skin together as the glue dries. Paint your whole face pale green.

5 Make dark gray shadows around your eyes and dark lines down from your nose to your chin. A touch of red on the fake scar adds a ghastly effect.

6 Cover your eyebrows with white triangles and paint long black eyelash lines. Make red lips with dots at each side of your mouth. Add lightning bolts to your cheeks.

31

Animal Faces

Shy Raccoon

Make a basic snout—paint your cheeks white before painting the whiskers on. Make a black raccoon mask around your eyes. Color your forehead and the sides of your face gray or brown.

Basic Snout

1 Make a white patch around your mouth. Use a paintbrush to draw a black or brown line down each side of your nose.

2 Paint the tip of your nose black. Make a black line under your nose down to the middle of your upper lip.

3 Extend the line both ways along your lip and curve it up. Paint a few dots on your upper lip and draw long whiskers onto your cheeks.

Design your own animal face. Look at a photograph of the animal and use some of the ideas here (it's fun to practice on dolls).

Ferocious Tiger

Make a basic snout without the whiskers. Paint white around your eyes. Color the rest of your face orange. Paint black stripes on your forehead and cheeks, and white fangs on your lower lip.

Friendly Panda

Make a basic snout but leave the whiskers off and don't paint the lines along your nose. Paint your cheeks and forehead white. Make big black patches around your eyes down onto your cheeks.

Curious Monkey

Paint white in kind of a heart shape up over your eyes and around your face. Color your forehead and the sides of your face brown. Outline your nose, nostrils, and mouth with black and make dark eyebrows.

Shine On

Experimenting with Media

Create a painting that sparkles without using paint or paper. "Paint" with tissue paper and glue onto aluminum foil for a picture so shiny and bright you'll need sunglasses to look at it!

Materials needed:

Wide paintbrush

Mixing dish and water

White glue

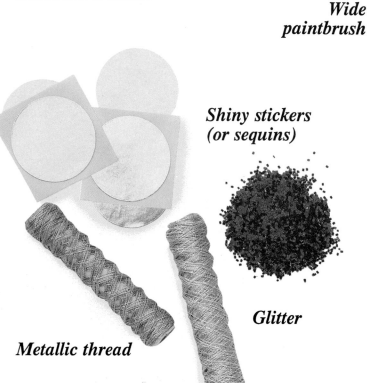

Shiny stickers (or sequins)

Glitter

Metallic thread

1 Mix equal amounts of glue and water. It looks milky white but will dry clear and shiny.

2 Spread out a piece of foil, shiny side up. Tear colored tissue paper into strips and pieces. Brush some glue mixture onto the foil.

3 Lay a piece of tissue paper down, then brush more glue over it. Keep adding tissue and glue, overlapping the tissue pieces to make a design.

Acrylic paints (optional)

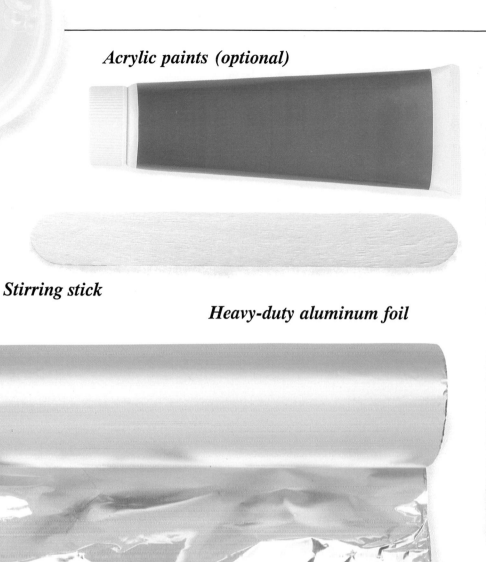

Stirring stick

Heavy-duty aluminum foil

Colored tissue paper

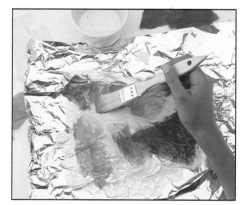

4 The tissue paper soaks up the wet glue and becomes your "paint." Create new colors where the tissue overlaps—even the glue turns colors.

5 Add shiny stickers, sequins, and metallic thread to make your painting sparkle. Use acrylic paints if you want some darker areas in your design.

6 Sprinkle glitter on top of your wet painting for a shimmery effect. When you're all finished, let your painting dry overnight.

Shiny Fun

Paint a picture or abstract design. Wrap the foil around sturdy cardboard to make a poster. Or cut small sections out of a big foil design and glue them onto folded construction paper to make shiny greeting cards.

Wrap your foil painting around a can to make a beautiful pencil holder or flower pot. Or use your sparkle painting to wrap a present—it's perfect for gifts you bake or make yourself.

Half and Half Paintings

Measuring Proportions

This project is a partnership between you and a photographer. Half of the picture is made up of photos cut out of a magazine, then you paint the other half. Try painting half a person or cartoon character. Or try using a black-and-white photo, mixing different shades of gray to match.

Materials needed:

Tempera paints and paintbrush

Pencil

Scissors

Old magazines

Heavy drawing paper and scrap paper

Glue

Cut photos out of old magazines and glue them on white paper. Draw light lines connecting them, being careful to make things the same size or *in proportion*.

Use tempera paints to color in the areas you've sketched. Mix the paint to match the colors in the photos. Test each color on scrap paper.

Watercolor Batik

Painting with Resists

Batik is the art of decorating cloth with *resist* designs. Part of the cloth is covered with wax or paste. The rest of the cloth is painted. The covered-up areas block out the paint—they resist being colored. After the paint has dried, the resist material is cleaned off and the un-colored cloth shines through.

Flour paste: (Ask an adult to help you.) Mix ½ cup white flour, ½ cup water, and 2 teaspoons alum (find alum where spices or medicines are sold). Using a blender works best—start with plain water, then slowly sprinkle in the flour and alum.

Watercolor paints

Materials needed:

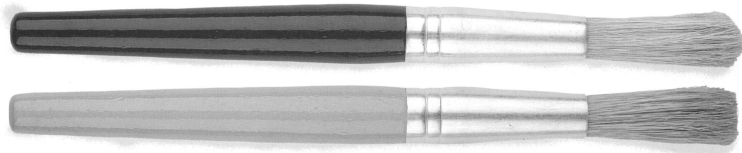

Brushes

Day One

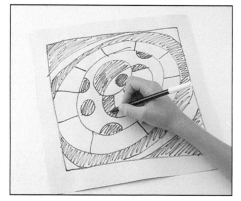

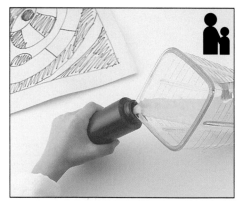

1 Plan your painting on scrap paper. Use your sketch as a guide when you "draw" with paste on the cloth.

2 Mix up a batch of flour paste and pour it into an empty squeeze bottle (a plastic ketchup bottle or dish soap bottle is fine).

3 Squeeze the paste onto the cloth following your design. You'll make interesting drips and blobs. Let it dry overnight.

9 × 12-inch (22 × 30 cm) prewashed white cloth

Squeeze bottle

Rinse water

Pencils and scrap paper

Day Two

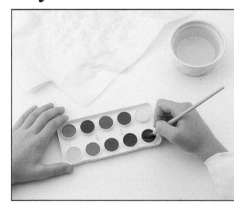

4 Place your cloth with its dried paste design on a pile of paper towels. Mix the colors you want for your painting.

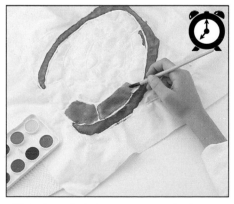

5 Paint the open areas of your cloth. The colors will look lighter as they dry, so use a lot of bright paint. Let it dry overnight.

Day Three

6 Work hard with your fingers to crack and rub the dried paste off the cloth. The strip of cloth beneath the paste resisted the color!

Finished Batiks

Ask a grown-up to help you iron the cloth if it's wrinkled. Abstract designs and simple picture batiks make beautiful works of art!

Batiks in Action

Shirt
Slip a pile of newspapers into a cotton T-shirt and batik the front. Use fabric paints so the colors won't wash out.

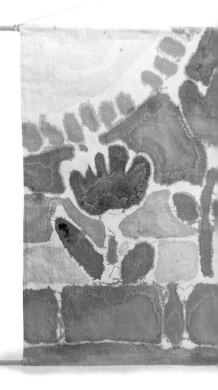

Pillow
Your batik can be made into a pillow with a bit of stitching and stuffing. Use fabric paints if you want your cloth to be washable.

Wall Hanging

Glue smooth dowels or natural twigs to the top and bottom edges of your batik. When the glue has dried, tie a string to the top stick for hanging.

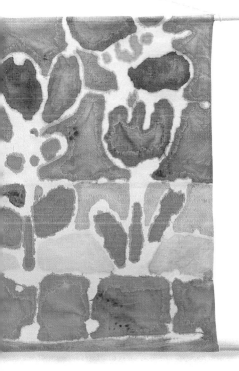

Resist Adventure

There are many other ways to experiment with resist painting. Here are two ways to try resist painting on paper instead of cloth. Any way you try it, it's fun to resist!

Crayon Resist

1 With a white crayon, draw a picture, message or abstract design on a piece of white paper.

2 Paint over your design with watercolors or tempera paint. The crayon resists being painted.

Glue Resist

1 Draw a design with white glue. Let it dry and then paint over it.

2 Use one color or a combination of beautiful colors. The glue resists the paint!

Paint Making

Making Paints and Pigments

Many years ago, artists had to make their own paints. You can make your own paint just because it's fun! Pretend you can't buy any ready-made paint. Experiment and invent different recipes and colors.

Materials needed:

Spoon

Containers

Mixing bowl
Water

Colored chalk (or powdered drink mix)

1 Powdered colors are called pigments. Make your own pigments by grinding colored chalk with stones.

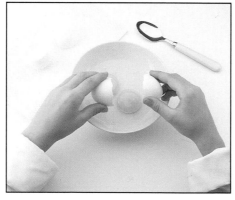

2 Crack two raw eggs into a bowl. Pour off the clear egg whites and save the yellow yolks.

3 Add a little bit of water and stir until you make a smooth, runny syrup. Pour it into several small containers.

Stones and paper plate

Vegetable oil

Pigments (bricks, dirt, or frozen berries)

Eggs

4 Add pigment to each dish to create the colors you want. Bright colors look the best—use powdered drink mix if you wish.

5 Paint with your egg tempera paint on heavy paper or cloth. Wash out the dishes before the egg mixture dries in them.

6 Don't stop with eggs! Ask for permission to paint with ketchup, mustard, orange juice, grape juice and more!

Prehistoric Paints

1 Pretend you're a caveman and collect samples of mud, dirt or pieces of brick. Look for lots of different colors.

2 Use stones to grind them into powder. For brighter colors, mash some frozen strawberries, blueberries or raspberries.

3 Mix oil with your pigments to make paints. Use a homemade brush and paint on a rock or piece of bark.

Part Two: Draw!

A Note to Grown-Ups

Draw! features ten unique drawing projects plus numerous variations. Young artists will love experimenting and developing their drawing skills while they're learning about important principles of art. Rather than drawing with only ordinary pencils and white drawing paper, they'll be encouraged to try charcoal pencils, colored pencils, felt-tip pens, crayons, pastel chalks and watercolor paints on everything from grocery bags to rolls of adding machine paper. All the while they will be learning about foreground and background, architecture and design, drawing a likeness and attention to detail, contour drawing, gesture drawing, animation, size, and drawing in 3-D.

Each project has a theme stated at the very beginning, and some projects suggest follow-up activities related to that theme. Some projects result in beautiful finished works to display or give away; others emphasize experimentation and the simple fun of *doing* them. They're all kid-tested to ensure success and inspire confidence.

Getting the Most Out of the Projects

While the projects provide clear instructions, photographs and lots of finished examples for ideas, each is open-ended so kids may decide what *they* want to draw. Some of the projects are easy to do in a short amount of time. Others require more patience and concentration.

While certain drawing tools are suggested for each project, children may enjoy experimenting with different ones. The projects are flexible to make it easy for you and your child to try as many activities as you wish. All the materials are inexpensive and are easy to find wherever school, art or office supplies are sold.

Some Drawing Tips for Kids

Draw every day! Even if it's for just a few minutes at a time, if you draw every day, you'll get better and better at it.

It's fun to draw from photos or use real models. It's fun to make stuff up and not look at anything while you draw. Try different ways and do what's best for you.

You can draw with long, smooth lines or you can make lots of little wispy lines. Draw realistic pictures or make fantasy, dreamlike drawings. There's no right or wrong way to draw!

Take a Line for a Walk

Contour Drawing

Contour is the outline of something, especially something curvy or odd shaped. Contour drawings are fun to do because they're fast and kind of wild looking—you don't have to be very careful. The idea is to observe very closely what you're drawing and draw quickly—just the shapes you see, not the details.

Warm Up—Abstract

Make a design with one long, twisty line. Start at one corner and walk your line all over the paper. Don't lift up your pencil until your design is completely finished—fill the whole page. Try drawing only straight lines, boxes and triangles. Then try one with curls and loops and zigzags.

1 Now try a real contour drawing. Pick an everyday object like a shoe, a toy, or a plant.

2 Draw the object with one long, twisty line. *Don't look at your paper* at all—really study the object you're drawing.

3 Draw the shapes you see. Draw the lines in the object. Don't lift your pencil or pen until your drawing is all done.

When you're finished drawing, look at what you've done. It's wild and beautiful, even if it doesn't look much like the object. Try another one!

Challenge yourself to do a contour drawing of an object with many different shapes and lines.

Anything you have around the house can be the subject of a contour drawing. Try doing lots of quick sketches.

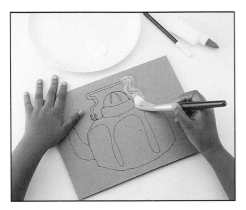

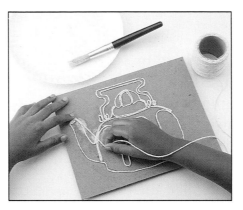

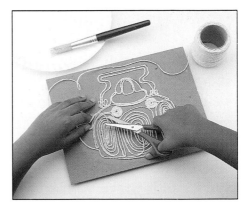

1 Now draw with one long line — of string! Sketch a picture on a piece of sturdy cardboard. Spread a thin layer of white glue all over it.

2 Stick the end of a piece of string down into the glue. Follow the lines of your sketch, pressing the string down as you go.

3 Use as much string as you can, making loops and swirls to fill in the shapes. If the glue dries, brush on some more.

Animal Scribbles

Gesture Drawings

Animals are fun to draw, but it can be hard to use a real animal as a model because they're always moving. To make realistic animal drawings, artists first make scribble drawings called *gesture drawings*. Doing gesture drawings of animals is a fast way of making sketches. All you have to do is make your scribbles look like the outline and main shapes of the animal. Don't bother with details, just scribble. Study what your animal looks like — then draw fast! It's fun to make lots of gesture drawings.

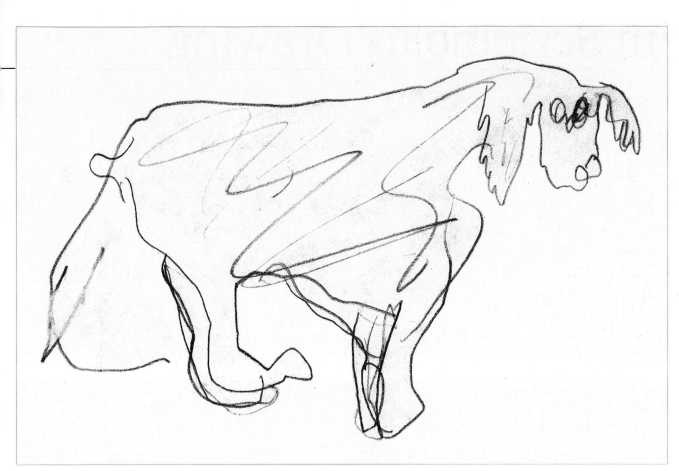

Start with an animal that's asleep. Then try doing a scribble while the animal is moving. Work fast! Your sketches don't have to be big and you can do one in less than a minute.

From Scribble to Drawing

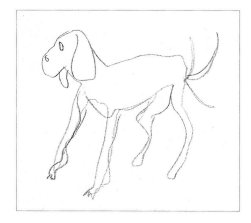

Pick one of your best scribbles to work on to make a finished drawing. Erase lines that you don't like. Draw heavier lines on top. Add eyes and whiskers; draw texture lines to show fur or feathers.

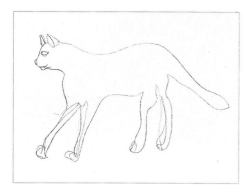

Add color or try drawing with a paintbrush and watery black paint. It's easy to make a great animal picture when you start with a scribble!

Close-Ups

Size

It's exciting to turn an everyday object — a shoe, backpack, phone or teddy bear — into an adventure scene! First make a large, detailed drawing. Then add teeny tiny people mountain climbing, skiing, horseback riding, mining coal — whatever you can think of.

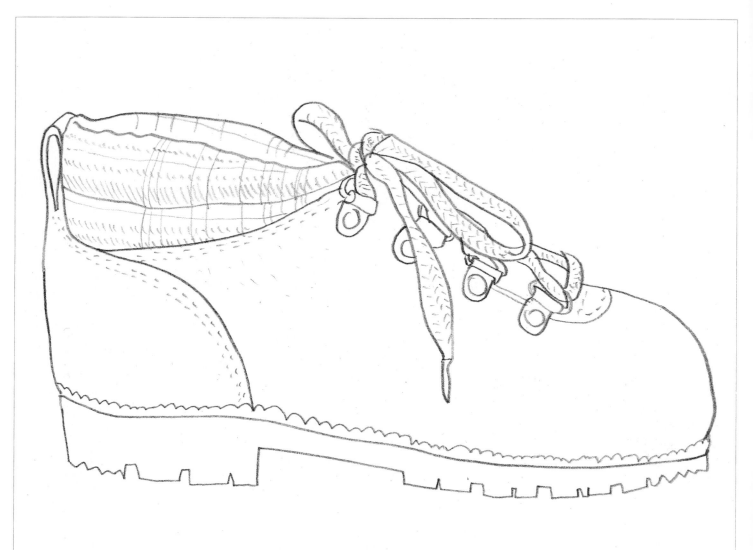

The little people will make the object you draw look huge! That's because you know how big people really are, so the object they're climbing on has to be so much bigger. This kind of size comparison is called *scale*.

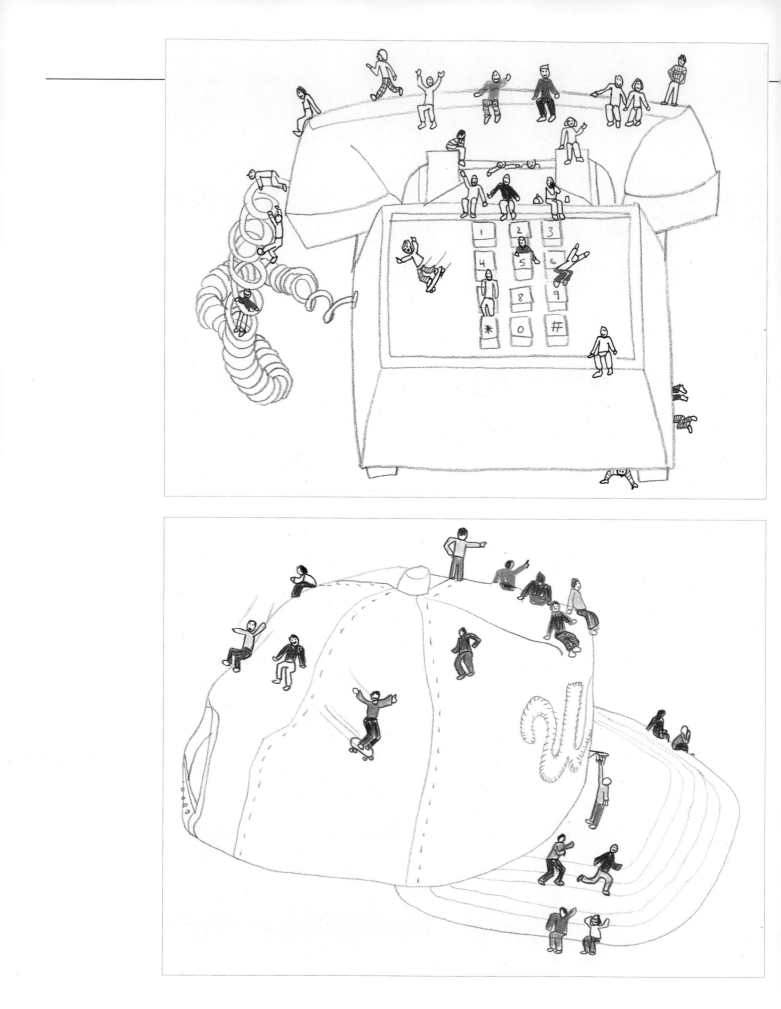

Upside Down

Drawing What You See

Drawing from an upside-down model sounds crazy, but try it and you'll be surprised how realistic your drawing will look. That's because you'll be drawing what you see, not what you think something should look like.

Pick a photograph, a picture in a magazine, or use your favorite cartoon character. Turn the picture upside down and draw what you see. Your drawing will be upside down, too!

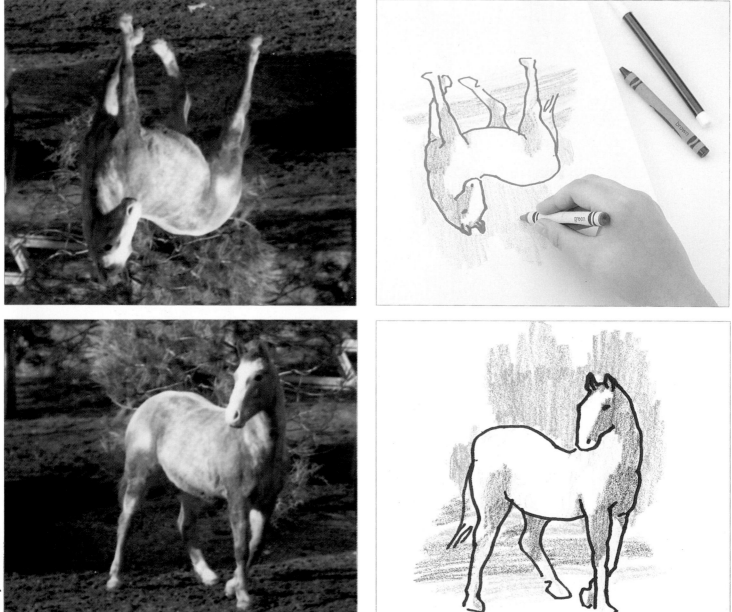

Be careful to make the lines in your drawing match the shapes you see in the photo. Add details, always working upside down. Look at the photo closely as you draw. Erase when you need to. Turn both pictures right side up when you're finished. How does it look now?

Photo by Fred W. Smith

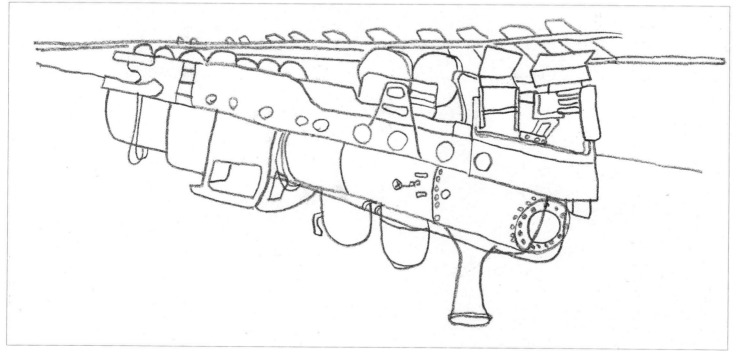

Inside Outside

Architecture and Design

If you could live anywhere you wanted, what would your house look like? Architecture is the art of making buildings. Pretend you're an architect and design your own home!

Draw the outside of your house. Make a first floor, a second floor and a roof. Add doors and windows, a garage, a greenhouse for plants, or a tower. If you run out of paper, tape another piece on and keep drawing.

Outside the house

Cut out your house. Cut the windows out and cut the doors on three sides so they'll open. Now flip the paper over and design the inside! Plan what each room will be, and draw stairs (or an elevator), furniture, curtains and decorations.

Inside the house

My Dream House

You can create a traditional house or a silly house. Make a tall townhouse or a house shaped like a triangle. Use your imagination!

Magic Tape

Foreground/Background

These tape pictures are magic! The trick is using *drafting* tape or *removable* tape (available at office supply stores). You put the tape down and draw *over* it—your drawing is "in front of" the tape. But when you peel the tape off, the white paper jumps *in front of* your drawing! The white paper becomes the *foreground* and your drawing becomes the *background*.

Use the tape to make a fancy zoo cage. Draw an animal on top of the tape, and when you peel it off, he'll be safely behind bars.

Spell out your name with cut pieces of tape. Color bright patterns over it, then pull up the tape to see your name jump to the foreground.

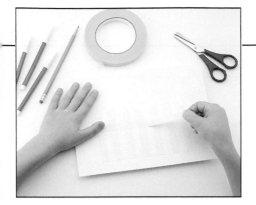

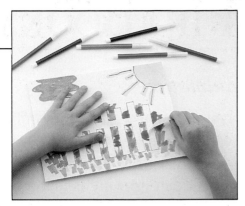

1 Draw a line for the ground and build a fence with tape. Use it off the roll or cut some pieces down the middle.

2 Use felt-tip pens to gently draw a garden. Draw tall flowers and little flowers, thick bushes and grass. Use lots of bright colors.

3 Pull up the tape. Now the fence is in the front! You can outline it in black and draw holes and cracks to make it look like wood.

Finished garden drawing

69

Flip Books

Animation

You can draw a movie! *Animation* means bringing your drawings to life. First make a little book, then draw a picture on each right-hand page. Each drawing is just a bit different from the drawing before it.

The secret to making a great flip book is to press hard with your pencil to make an impression on the page *underneath* the page you're working on. Using the impression as a guide, the pictures will be in the same place on each page. Try the story ideas shown here, or make up your own.

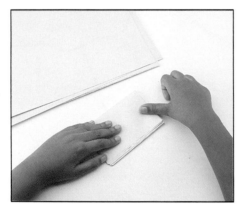

1 Fold two pieces of plain paper in half the long way. Fold them in half again across the middle, then fold them once more.

2 Unfold the last two folds and cut four sections along the fold marks. Slip these sections into each other to make a book.

3 Staple the pages together on the fold. Trim the outside edges so the pages are even.

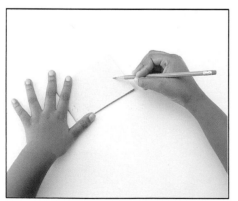

4 Start with a very simple "story": a bubble getting bigger and bigger until it pops. On the first page, draw the bubble as a tiny dot.

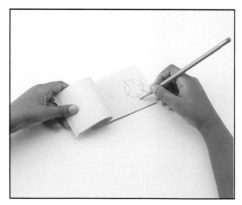

5 Draw the bubble bigger on each page. Toward the end, sketch the biggest bubble with lines bursting out from the middle.

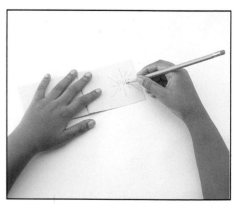

6 On the last page, draw only the bursting lines with the word "POP" right in the middle. Now try a story with more action.

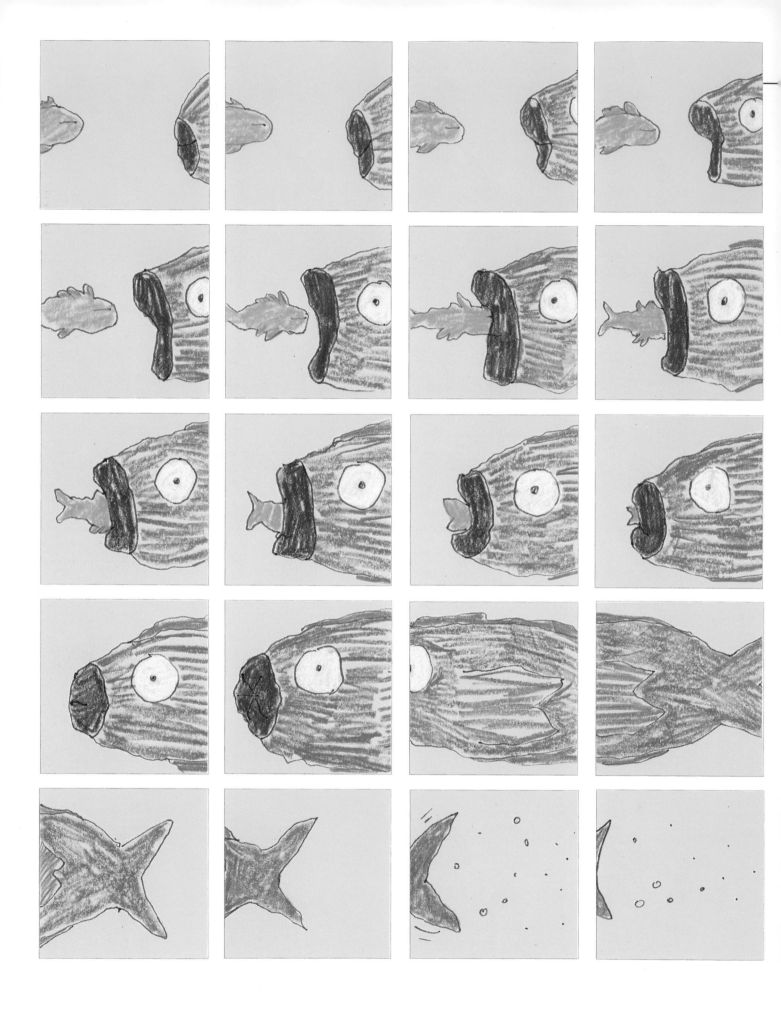

Daring Drawing

Experimenting with Tools and Techniques

Drawing doesn't have to be done with ordinary pencils on regular paper. Try drawing with light-colored pencils or chalks on dark paper. Draw with cotton-tip swabs dipped in a colored soft drink. Pretend your pencil is so heavy you can hardly lift it. Or try any of these daring drawing adventures.

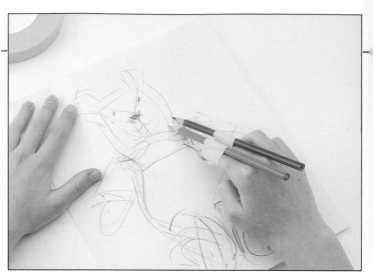

Robot Fingers. Draw with a pencil taped onto your finger, or tape colored pencils onto two fingers.

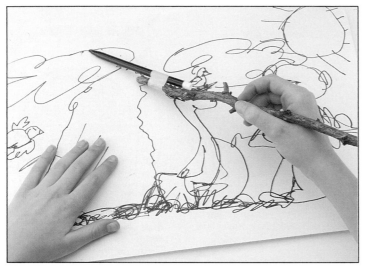

Stick with It. Tape a pencil or felt-tip pen onto a stick and draw on large pieces of paper.

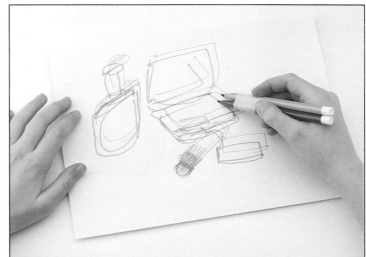

Double Fun. Tape two pencils or felt-tip pens together and make a drawing with double lines.

No Peeking. Make a drawing with a towel covering your hand!

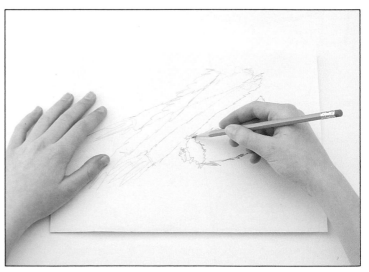

Shaky Pencil. Pretend your pencil has the jitters—or the hiccups. You can barely control it enough to draw!

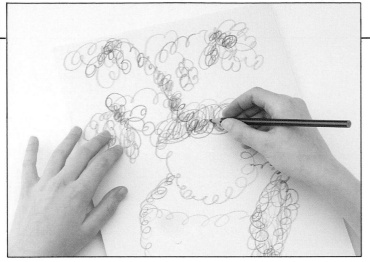

Dizzy Pencil. Pretend your pencil is so dizzy it keeps making loops and circles as you draw.

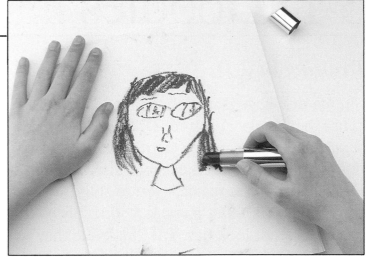

Lip-Smacking Good. Get permission to draw with an old tube of lipstick.

You're in the Driver's Seat. Make a drawing with a toy car run through paint or chalk dust.

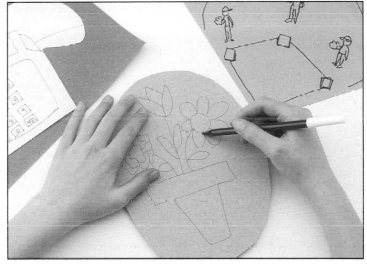

Cut Paper Drawings. Draw on construction paper cut into shapes like circles, stars and diamonds.

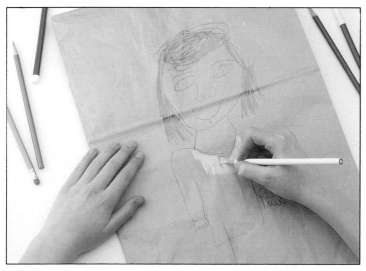

It's in the Bag. Try drawing on grocery store bags—which drawing instrument will you use?

It Adds Up. Use long rolls of adding machine paper for a long drawing or *mural*.

3-D Doodles

Drawing in 3-D

Simple drawings like stick figures look flat because they're *two dimensional*: They don't show *depth*. Being able to show depth means drawing not just the front of objects but also the sides. Drawing in 3-D is magic—you're still drawing simple lines on a flat page, but suddenly your drawings don't look flat. They look like they're jumping off the paper at you!

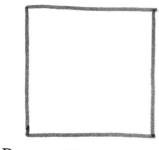

1 Draw a square.

2 Make a line like this for the back edge of the box.

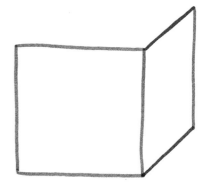

3 Draw two slanted lines to finish the side.

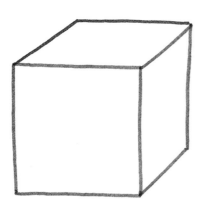

4 Finish the box top with these two lines.

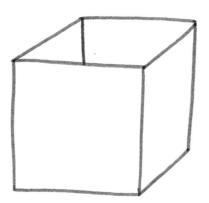

5 For a box open at the top, draw a line like this.

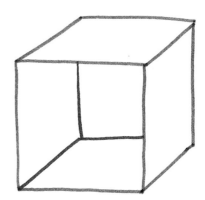

6 For a box open in the front, draw these lines.

Box doodle.

Box open at the top.

Box open in the front.

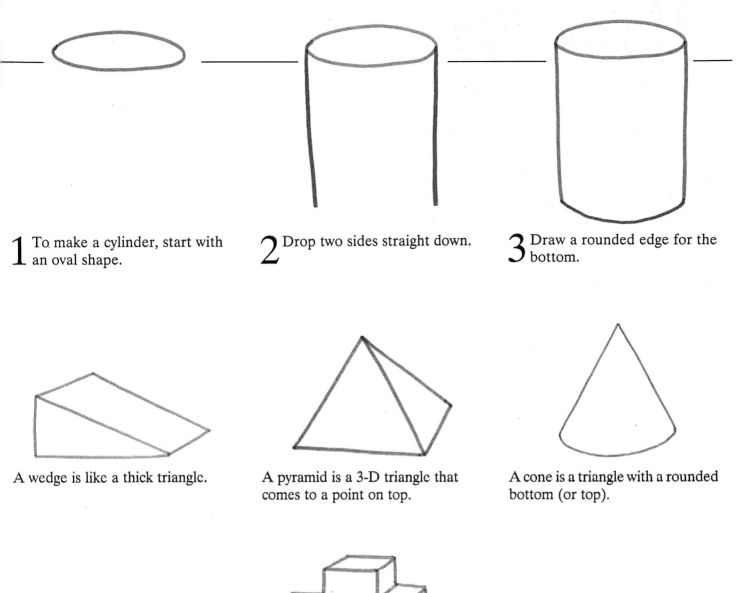

1 To make a cylinder, start with an oval shape.

2 Drop two sides straight down.

3 Draw a rounded edge for the bottom.

A wedge is like a thick triangle.

A pyramid is a 3-D triangle that comes to a point on top.

A cone is a triangle with a rounded bottom (or top).

Add depth to any shape by adding lines to show the back edges and sides.

Cylinder doodle.

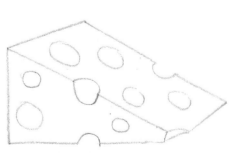

Wedge doodle.

Building doodle.

Shading Doodles

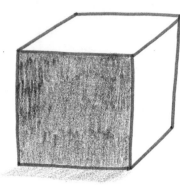 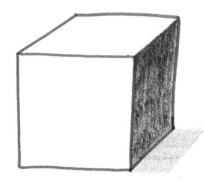 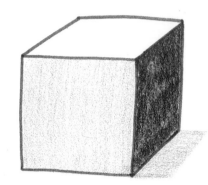

1 You can show depth by adding shading and shadows.

2 Pick a side to be in the shade and make that side dark.

3 Add even more depth by shading another side lighter.

  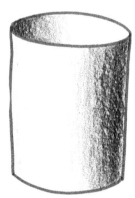

1 Shading wraps around a curved surface in a *blended tone*.

2 Make the shade dark in the back and lighter in the front.

3 To make the cylinder look open, shade part of the top oval.

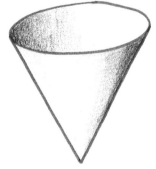  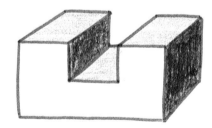

Use these rules to shade any shape.

Pick a *light source* and always shade the opposite side.

Use the same shading for all the sides that face the same way.

 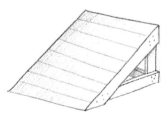 

Long Doodles

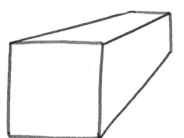
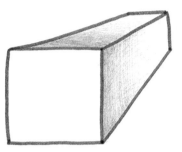

1 To make a long box, draw a big square and a tiny square.

2 Draw three long lines and erase the inside edges.

3 Add shading for a long 3-D box.

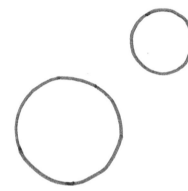

1 For a cylinder, make a big front circle and a tiny back circle.

2 Draw two long lines and erase the bottom of the back circle.

3 Shade it dark on the bottom and lighter in the middle.

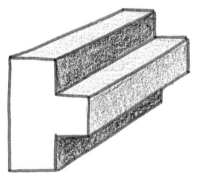
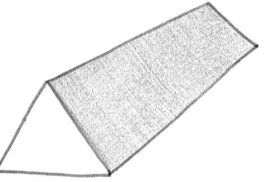

You can make any shape look long.

Remember that things look smaller the farther away they are.

So make the back end much smaller than the front end.

79

3-D Letters

  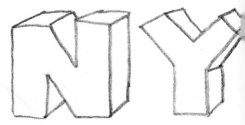

It's fun to add back edges and slanted sides to make 3-D letters.

Start with block letters that have all straight edges.

Draw lightly at first so you can erase any lines that aren't needed.

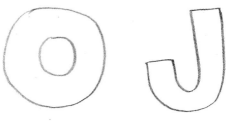 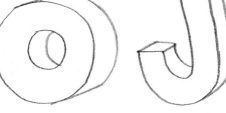 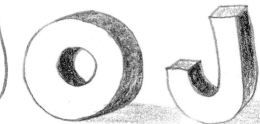

Now try making curved letters. Add shading and shadows!

 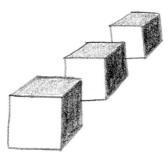 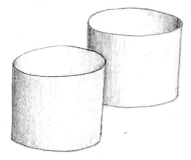

Make things look closer or farther away by overlapping them.

Make things look even farther away by drawing them smaller.

Do the same thing with any shapes! Add shading.

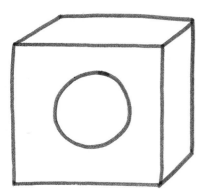

1 Create depth by showing thickness. Draw a circle on a box.

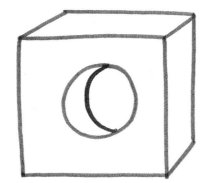

2 Draw a moon shape to make the inside edge of the circle.

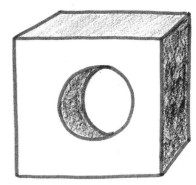

3 Add shading for a 3-D window.

Show thickness in doorways and arches the same way.

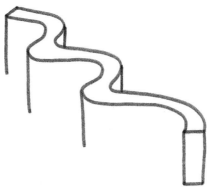

Make a wavy wall: Draw a wiggly path. Draw lines down for sides.

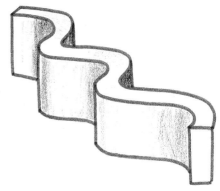

Make a bottom edge to match the top and add shading.

Use the same technique to make cliffs or flags.

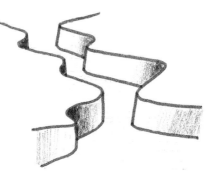

3-D Drawings

You can combine shapes and techniques like overlapping, shading, and showing thickness to make wonderful 3-D drawings. Use your imagination to create realistic drawings as well as fantasy drawings. Sketch and erase, draw and shade.

My Self-Portrait

Drawing a Likeness

A self-portrait is a picture you draw of yourself as you look in a mirror. Sit in front of a mirror at a table or vanity, or use a clipboard under your paper. Study how you look in the mirror. Reach up and feel your face. What is it about your face that makes you look like you?

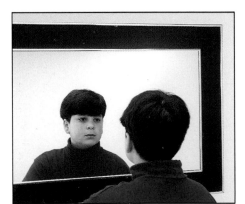

1 Take a close look at yourself. The front view of your head is an oval or egg shape, and your face takes up only the lower part of that shape.

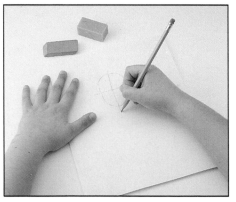

2 Draw the outside shape of your head. Make light guidelines through the middle of this shape, from top to bottom and side to side.

3 Sketch your eyes on the line that goes across. Above the eyes, draw your eyebrows and hair. *Look!* Your hair and forehead take more room than you think!

How much space is between your eyes and your eyebrows?

What shape is the area under your nose and above your lips?

Don't worry about making mistakes. You can always draw yourself again. The more you draw, the better you'll get at making things look real.

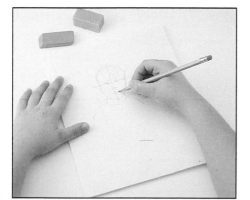

4 Below the eyes, sketch your nose, mouth and chin. Draw your ears at the same level as your nose, and your neck almost as wide as your face.

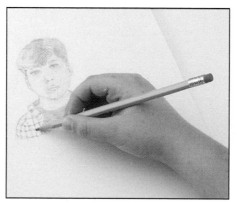

5 Erase your guidelines and draw each part of your face more carefully. Draw with smooth, strong lines. How wide is your mouth? How big are your ears?

6 Keep looking back and forth from the mirror to the drawing paper. Close one eye and measure your reflection with your fingers.

Look at Me

How do you make your self-portrait
look like *you*? Draw what you see, not
what you think you should look like.

My Profile

A profile is a head seen from the side. You only see one eye, one ear, one side of the nose and mouth. Have an adult help you set up two mirrors so they meet and make a corner. Sit facing one of the mirrors and you'll see your profile in the other.

Can you grin? Can you frown? Can you look angry, sad, surprised, scared or worried? Draw yourself making as many different faces as you can.

Hair is fun to draw! You can't draw every single strand of hair, so look for the edges. Draw the lines where hair meets skin, and where it curls and overlaps.

1 Take a close look—notice how much of your profile is hair! Your face takes up only part of one side. Draw the shape of your head.

2 Make light guidelines through the middle. Draw your eye on the line that goes across. It looks like a triangle with top and bottom eyelids and eyelashes.

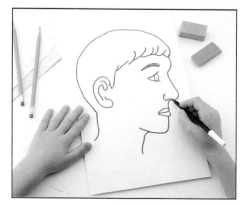

3 Sketch the other features of your face. Then erase the guidelines and finish your drawing by adding details to your eye, nose, lips, eyebrow and hair.

Dress Up to Draw

Wear hats and scarves, jewelry and wild hairstyles when you draw yourself. Drawing costumes adds lots of fun to self-portraits.

Bright Idea

Set up a lamp beside you so that the bright light falls on one side of your face. Draw yourself and the dark shadows that the light creates on your face.

Block Heads

Once you get good at drawing your self-portrait, construct a 3-D portrait! Draw a front view of your face, a profile of each side, then fill in the top and the back (mostly hair!). Tape them together for a funny portrait sculpture.

Part Three: Make Prints!

A Note to Grown-Ups

Make Prints! features eleven unique printing projects plus numerous variations. Young artists will love doing these activities even while they're learning basic principles of art and print-making. In traditional projects—as well as some unconventional ones—they'll be printing with found objects from around the house and yard, bars of soap and wood blocks, erasers, melted crayons, silk screens, vegetables, and perhaps the simplest tools of all, their fingers! All the while they'll be exploring patterns and shapes, textures, spontaneous design, and positive and negative space.

Each project has a theme, stated at the very beginning, and some projects suggest follow-up activities related to that theme. Some projects result in beautiful finished works to display or give away; others emphasize experimentation and the simple fun of doing them. They're all kid-tested to ensure success and inspire confidence.

Getting the Most Out of the Projects

Each project is both fun to do and educational. While the projects provide clear step-by-step instructions and photographs, each is open-ended so kids may decide what they want to print. Some of the projects are easy to do in a short amount of time. Others require more patience and even adult supervision.

The list of materials shown at the beginning of each activity is for the featured project only. Suggested alternatives may require different supplies. Feel free to substitute! For example, almost all of the projects that call for a brayer and printing ink can also be done with tempera paint and sponge pieces. The projects offer flexibility to make it easy for you and your child to try as many activities as you wish.

Collecting Supplies

All of the projects can be done with household items or inexpensive, easy-to-find supplies (see pages 5-6 for definitions of any art materials you're not already familiar with). Here are some household items you'll want to make sure you have on hand: newspapers, scrap cardboard, an old cookie sheet, old crayons, string, liquid laundry starch, aluminum foil, sponges, paper towels, masking tape.

Printmaking Tips for Kids

You'll create lots of prints. Make a clothesline out of string and plastic clothes-pins so you can hang wet prints to dry.

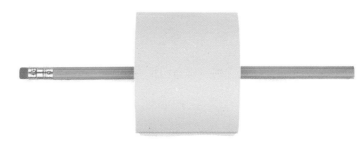

You can make your own brayer! Cover a roll of adding machine paper with clear tape and stick a pencil down the middle for a handle. Hold it like a rolling pin and you're ready to roll!

Collections

Studying Patterns and Shapes

What do clothespins, thread spools, bottle caps
and hair curlers have in common? Answer:
They all make great Collection Prints.

Materials needed:

*Tempera paint
(or water-based ink)*

Things to print wit

White or colored paper

Newspaper or scrap paper

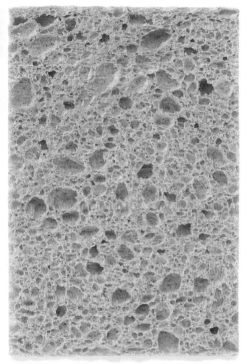

Pieces of sponge (or brayer)

1 Collect things that have interesting shapes. Make sure they can be washed clean or thrown away after you print with them.

2 You'll use several methods to print with the things in your collection. Lay big, flat things like lace on a piece of scrap paper.

3 Use a sponge to pat on paint (or use a brayer to roll ink). Move the painted object onto a piece of clean scrap paper, lay white paper on top and rub.

4 For small, hard objects use sponge pieces, a brayer or your fingers to spread on a thin coat of paint or ink. Then stamp the object down on your white paper.

5 Some things like string or chains can be dipped into a bowl of paint, then laid out carefully on clean scrap paper. Lay your printing paper on top and press.

6 Soft things can be dabbed into paint that's been spread thin on a plate. Pat them into the paint a few times, then stamp them onto your printing paper.

Collecting Fun

Print different things on one sheet of white paper to make a collage. Print the largest things first, then the smaller things on top or next to them. If you use different colors, let each color dry before going on.

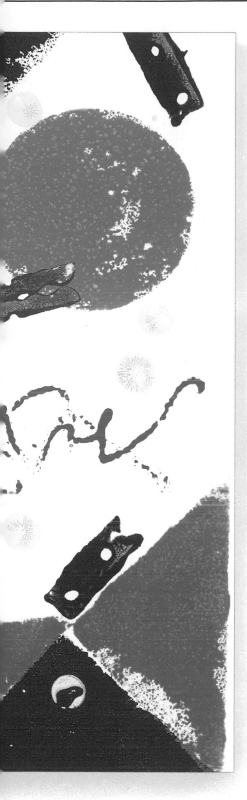

Print lots of things on different papers, then cut them out when they're dry. Glue the cut-out prints on another paper to create a design.

Use the things in your collection to build a picture! In this example, a bottle cap is the dog's body, a key makes the man's arms, and a piece of string printed the leash.

Prints Charming

Making a Monoprint

"Mono" is a Latin word meaning one. In this project you'll make one print of each painting you create. It's fun to try different color and texture combinations!

Tempera paint

Materials needed:

Paintbrush

White paper

Old cookie sheet

Liquid laundry starch

1 Pour a little starch onto the cookie sheet. Add one or more colors of paint.

2 Make swirls of color, blend colors together, or drip and splatter dots of paint.

3 Lay a piece of paper on top. Gently rub, then lift the paper to see your print. Wipe the cookie sheet clean and start another!

Charming Monoprints

Place cut or torn pieces of paper and leaves over your painting before you lay the white paper on top. This will block part of the paint and make interesting designs.

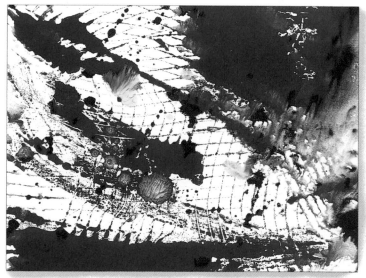

Collect objects to make textures in your painting — drag a comb through it, dab a crumpled piece of aluminum foil on it, or drive a toy car through it!

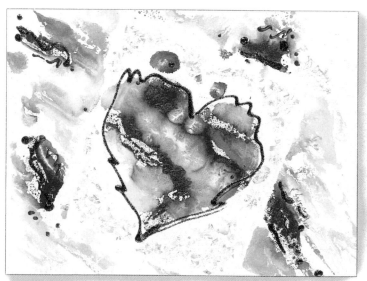

Add glitter while the paint is wet, and felt pen lines after it's dry. Make a realistic picture if you wish — but keep your subject simple.

Monoprint Drawing

1 Roll a *thin* layer of water-based printing ink onto a cookie sheet with a brayer. Use one color or roll on several colors.

2 Gently lay a piece of white paper on top of the ink. Use a pencil to draw a picture on the paper. Press hard!

3 When you're finished drawing, lift the paper to see your print on the bottom side!

Nature Prints

Seeing Invisible Textures

You can capture the beautiful textures of nature with these fast and simple prints. Leaves, pine needles, feathers, flowers, seaweed and even fish make wonderful designs.

Materials needed:

Cotton

Paintbrushes

Paper towels

Print a Fish

1 Clean your fish with a damp paper towel. If the insides have been removed, stuff it with paper towels so its belly is round and firm.

2 Lay the fish on a piece of cardboard. Spread out the tail and fins and pin them down or prop them up with bits of paper towel.

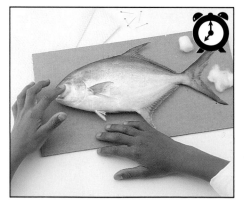

3 Cover the eye with a little piece of cotton and let your fish dry for two hours before going on.

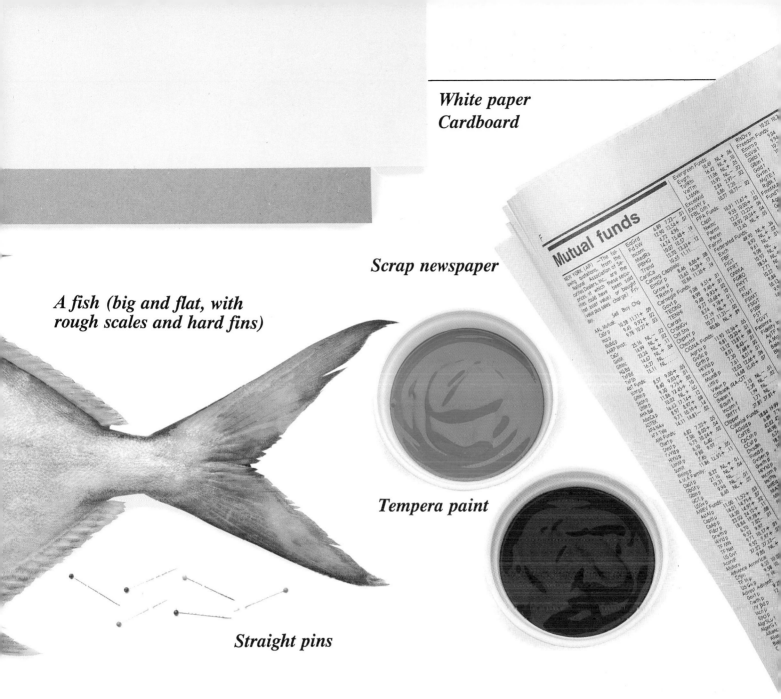

White paper
Cardboard

Mutual funds

Scrap newspaper

A fish (big and flat, with rough scales and hard fins)

Tempera paint

Straight pins

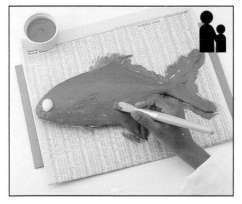

4 Pull the pins out and slip newspaper under your fish. Brush a layer of thick tempera paint onto the fish.

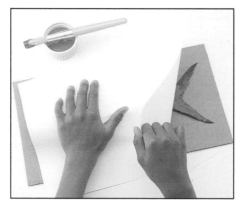

5 Pull out the newspaper and lay white paper on the painted fish. Carefully rub all over the fish, especially its face, fins and tail.

6 Lift the paper to see your print! After your print is dry, use a thin brush to paint in an eye and touch up areas that didn't print well.

Natural Textures

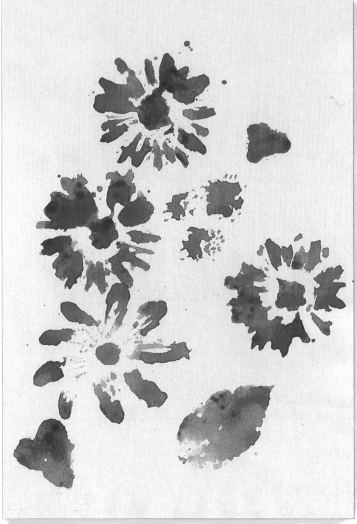

Brush Prints

Hold a flower or feather on newspaper and brush a layer of tempera paint on top. Set the painted flower or feather on a clean piece of newspaper, paint side up. Lay a piece of white paper on top and rub gently.

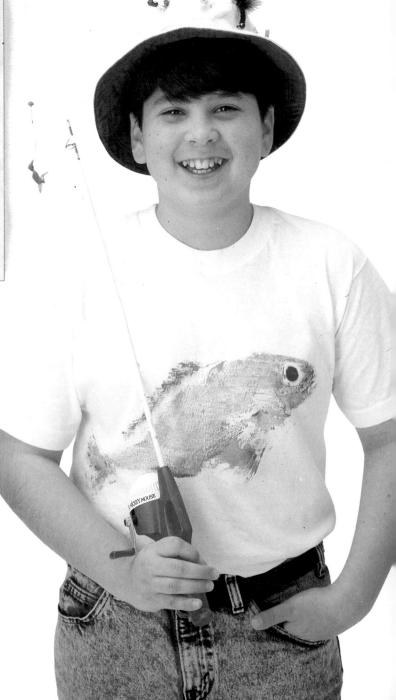

Fishy Shirts

Print a fish right onto a T-shirt or sweatshirt. Use fabric paint so the fish won't come out in the wash!

Brayer Prints

Hold a leaf by its stem on a piece of newspaper. Roll ink all over one side. Lay the leaf on white paper, ink side down. Cover with clean newspaper and rub.

Negative Leaves

Lay a piece of paper on the bottom of a big box. Place several leaves on the paper. Dip a toothbrush into paint, hold it down in the box, and rub your thumb over the bristles to splatter the paint. Keep going until the leaves and paper are covered with dots.

Symmetrical Prints

Creating Spontaneous Designs

These prints are almost like accidents: You don't plan them out, you just let them happen—and they're beautiful! Because you fold a piece of paper and then unfold it, the design is symmetrical, meaning it's the same on both sides of the fold.

Materials needed:

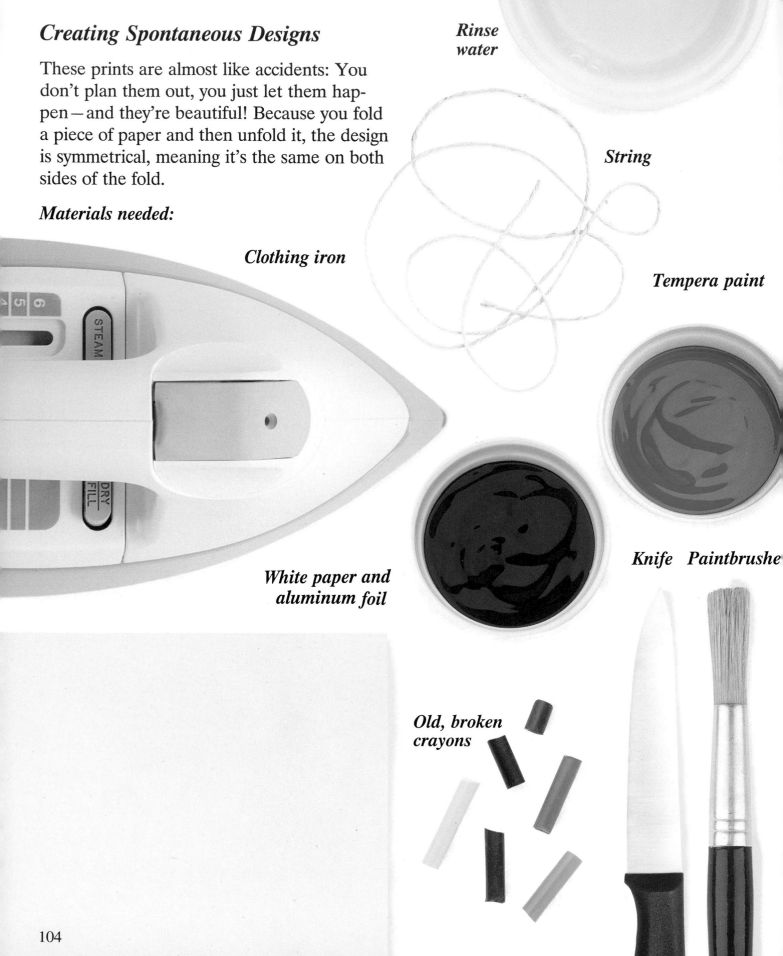

Rinse water

String

Clothing iron

Tempera paint

White paper and aluminum foil

Knife   Paintbrushe

Old, broken crayons

Crayon Melts

1 Peel the paper off old, broken crayons and have an adult chop them into tiny pieces. Fold a piece of paper in half, then open it.

2 Arrange bits of crayon on one side of the paper to make a design. Carefully fold your paper again, bringing the blank half over on top of the crayon design.

3 Cover the bottom of an iron with foil before turning it on. Have an adult iron the folded paper. Unfold the paper while it's still hot to see the melted design inside.

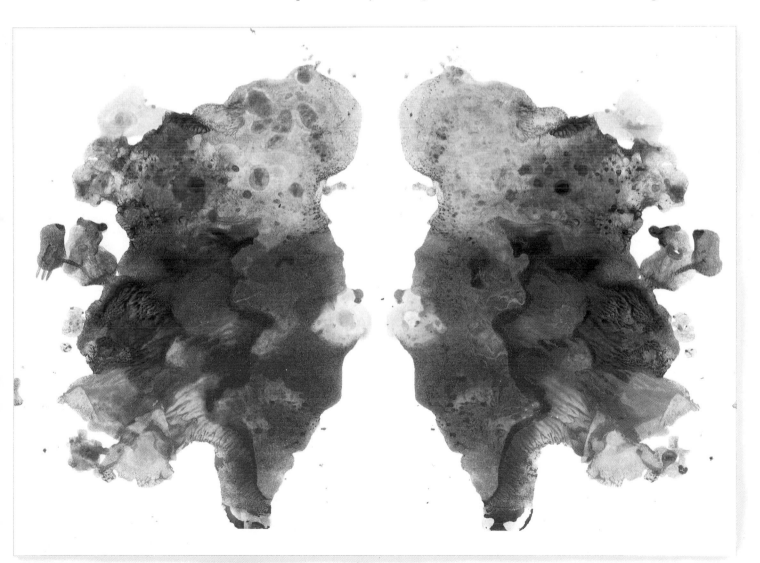

Double Designs

1 Fold a paper in half, then open it. Brush, drip and splatter paints on one side of the fold. Rinse your brush after each color.

2 When you're done painting, fold the paper, rub gently, then unfold it to see your colorful two-sided print!

String Pulls

1 Fold a paper in half, then open it. Dip an 18″ (45 cm) piece of string into a bowl of paint, holding on to one clean end.

2 Lay the paint-covered string on one side of the paper, looping and curling it around. Fold the paper again and hold it down.

3 Pull the string out and unfold the paper to see your design. Let one color dry, then do another string with a different color.

4 Or, for a different look, set up several painted strings at the same time, fold the paper, and pull them out one by one.

Make an abstract double design with colorful drips and splatters.

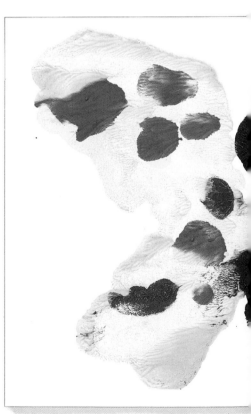

Butterflies, flowers, and apples are good subjects for Double Designs.

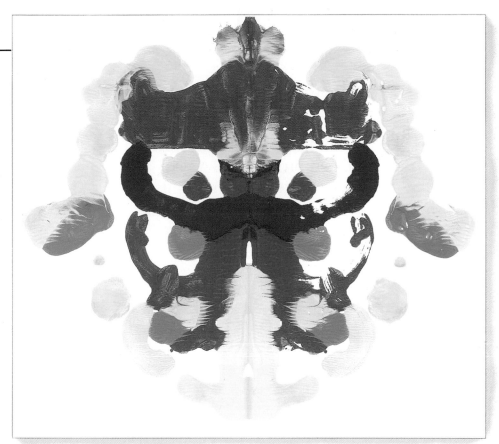

Make a realistic picture. Paint half the picture on one side of the fold—folding and pressing creates the whole design.

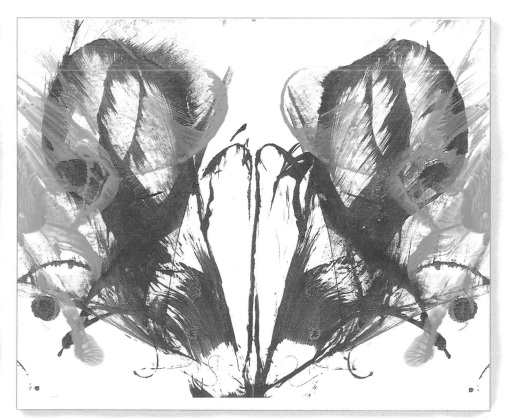

Do many different String Pulls—try pulling fast and pulling slowly. Experiment with thread, yarn, ribbon, jewelry chains.

Hammered Wood

Making a Wood Block

You'll get some exercise as you pound designs into wood with a hammer! Using wood blocks is a very traditional and professional way of printing. Wood blocks make beautiful prints because you can engrave thin lines and interesting patterns in them, and the natural wood grain adds a special look.

Old, weathered wood

Materials needed:

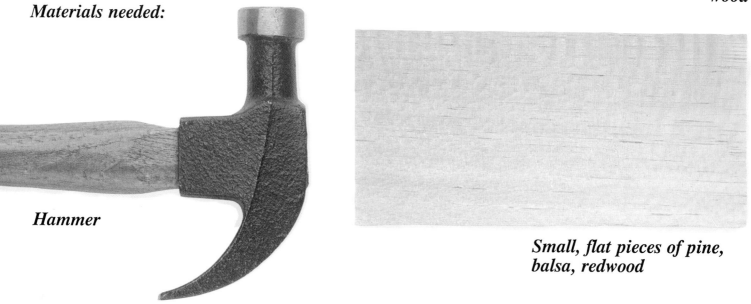

Hammer

Small, flat pieces of pine, balsa, redwood

Pencil

1 Collect pieces of metal with interesting shapes—get permission to use them! Ask an adult to help you if you've never used a hammer before.

2 Hold a metal tool against the wood and hit it with a hammer. Experiment! Some tools need only a soft tap; others need to be pounded hard.

Caution! Work slowly and be very careful not to hurt yourself with the hammer or metal tools. Cover machine parts and gears with a cloth before hammering them.

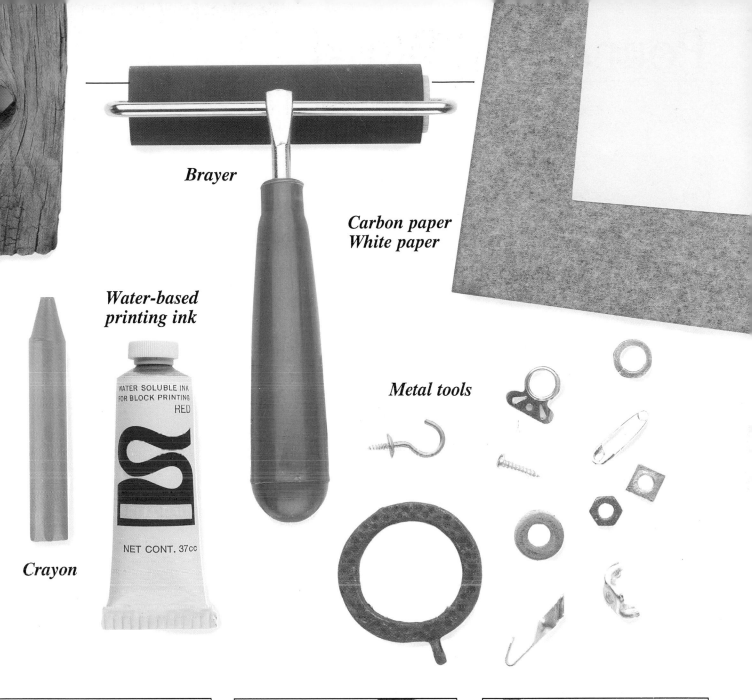

Brayer

**Carbon paper
White paper**

**Water-based
printing ink**

WATER SOLUBLE INK
FOR BLOCK PRINTING
RED

NET CONT. 37cc

Metal tools

Crayon

4 Test your block before printing:
Lay a piece of paper on top and
rub with a crayon to see how your
design will look.

5 When you're happy with your
design, roll a thin layer of ink on
your block. Put a piece of paper on
top and rub hard with your fingers.

6 To print a realistic picture, draw
it on paper first. Use carbon
paper to transfer your sketch onto
the wood and then engrave your
design with metal tools.

Pounded Patterns

If your design has words or numbers in it, make them *backwards* on your block so they'll print the right way.

Tap on the handle of a flat screwdriver to make a little line. Move it just a bit and tap it again, move it and tap, move it and tap, to cut a straight or curved line.

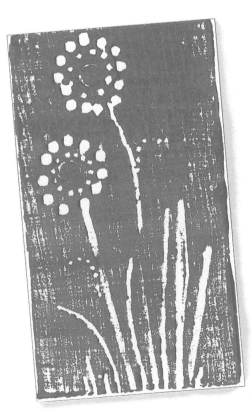

Use different tools to make different patterns. Nails will make little round holes. The end of a bolt can make a square or hexagon.

This coyote was printed with a block made of styrofoam pieces glued onto heavy cardboard.

Styrofoam Blocks

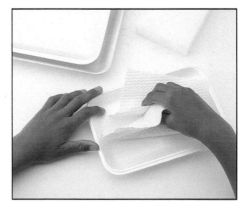

1 Find an old block of styrofoam packing material, or clean off the styrofoam tray from a package of meat or fruit.

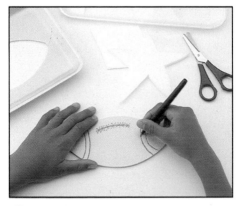

2 Cut shapes out of the foam and "carve" or draw designs into it with a ball-point pen. Press hard.

3 When your design is finished, roll on some ink, lay a piece of paper on top, and rub over it with your fingers to make a print.

Fingerprinting

Printing a Story

Make dozens of characters and pictures with tools you always have on hand—your fingers! You can even create your own cartoon strips.

Materials needed:

White paper

Washable ink pad

Felt-tip pen

Tempera paint

1 Make lots of fingerprints by touching the ink with your finger, then pressing it onto the paper. Wash your hands while the fingerprints dry.

2 Using a felt pen, add eyes, smiles, arms and legs, hair and clothes to make people! You can also create animal characters.

3 Have fun creating comic strips! Show motion by drawing lines around your characters. Make them talk or think by adding balloons or bubbles with words in them.

Animal Tracks

Carving a Likeness

Who walked all over the writing paper? Who left their footprints on the birthday presents? Here's how to make fancy designs with the tracks of your favorite animals.

Materials needed:

Ink pad

Hobby knife

Eraser

Felt-tip pens

Paper

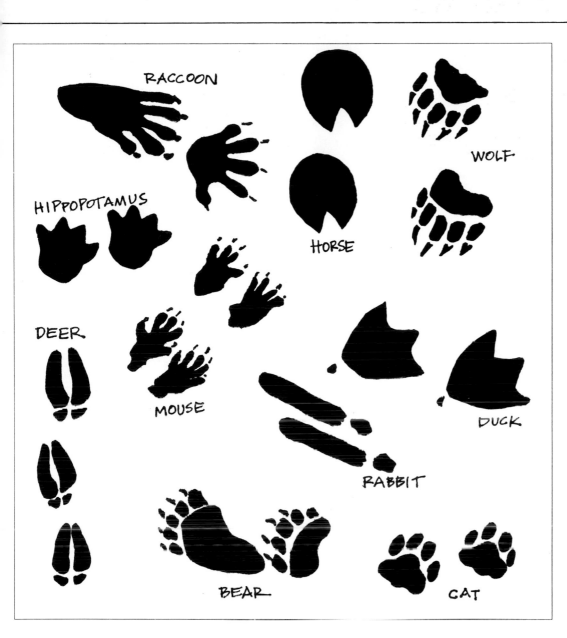

RACCOON

WOLF

HIPPOPOTAMUS

HORSE

DEER

MOUSE

DUCK

RABBIT

BEAR

CAT

Find out what your favorite animal's track looks like. If it isn't shown here, go to the library and ask for a field guide to animal tracks.

1 Make a small drawing of a footprint on one side of an eraser with a felt pen. Keep your drawing very simple.

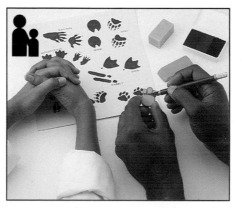

2 Have an adult help you cut *around* your drawing. Carve down at least ¼ inch (½ cm) or carve away the whole eraser.

3 Stamp the carved eraser footprint onto the ink pad and press it onto your paper. Check the design and carve more if you need to.

Animal Track Treasures

Carefully stamp blown-up balloons — wow!

Use fabric paints or latex house paints to decorate T-shirts. This track was made with a potato stamp.

Throw a wildlife party! Stamp invitations, gift cards and thank you cards.

Make wrapping paper by stamping shelf paper or newsprint.

Take your animal for a walk across writing paper to make stationery.

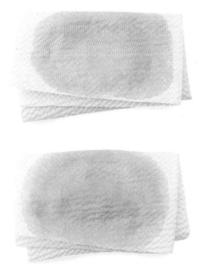

Make colorful ink pads!
Fold up pieces of paper towel and drip food coloring on top.

Footprint variations

There's more than one way to make animal tracks. Get permission and have an adult help you with these footprinting projects.

Pet Prints

1 Use *nontoxic* paint to collect prints of gentle pets like your dog or cat. Spread a thin layer of paint on a paper plate.

2 Press the animal's paw into the paint, then onto the paper. Wipe the paw as clean as you can with wet paper towels.

Potato Paws

1 Cut a potato in half and dry it. Draw a footprint onto the cut surface with a felt pen. Have an adult carve all around your track.

2 Dip the stamp into a shallow dish of paint, or paint just the footprint with a paintbrush, and then stamp it.

Rubbings

Working with Textures and Impressions

If you look carefully, you can find interesting textures all around you: in car tires and tennis shoe soles, wood and tile walls and floors, tree bark, wicker and cloth. It's fun to collect these patterns and designs by making rubbings.

Materials needed:

Masking tape

Textured objects

White paper

Dark crayons with the paper peeled off

1 Lay a piece of paper on top of the object you want an impression of. Don't let the paper wiggle — use tape to hold it in place.

2 Rub over the object gently with the side of a crayon. Practice making it lighter or darker until you can really see the bumpy patterns.

3 Try using different colors. You'll see textures in the rubbings that you'd never notice just looking at the objects!

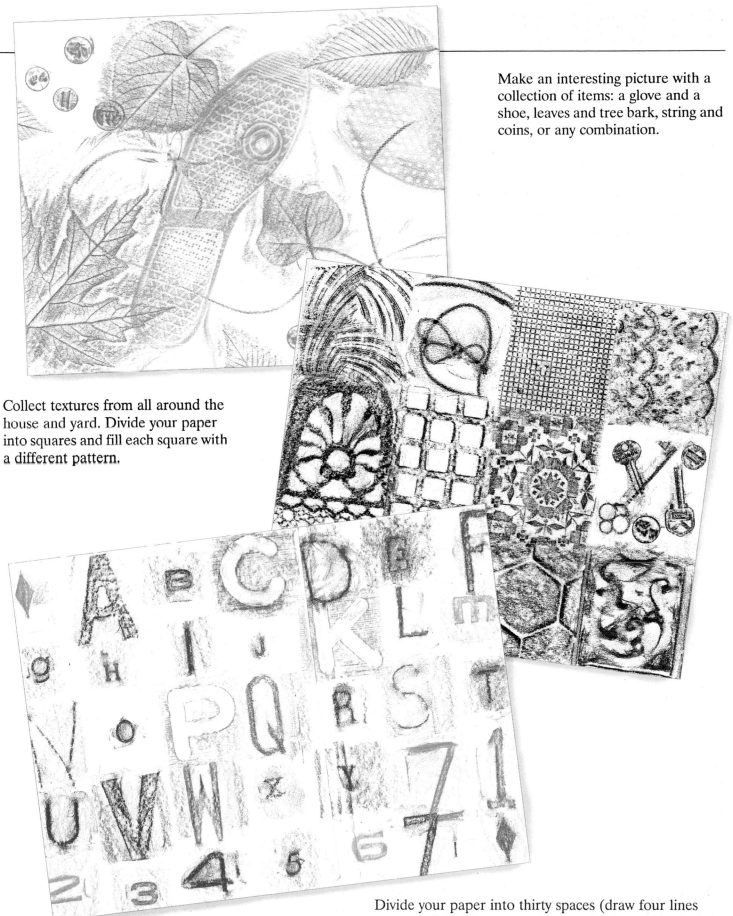

Make an interesting picture with a collection of items: a glove and a shoe, leaves and tree bark, string and coins, or any combination.

Collect textures from all around the house and yard. Divide your paper into squares and fill each square with a different pattern.

Divide your paper into thirty spaces (draw four lines across and five lines up and down). Make rubbings of the alphabet from mailboxes, cars, shoes and signs.

Veggie Geometry

Repetition in Design

Vegetables are good for you — if you're a print-maker! Slice a vegetable or a piece of fruit in half to reveal an interesting design inside. Then use them to print a repeating pattern, or use the shapes to create a picture.

Materials needed:

Sponge pieces

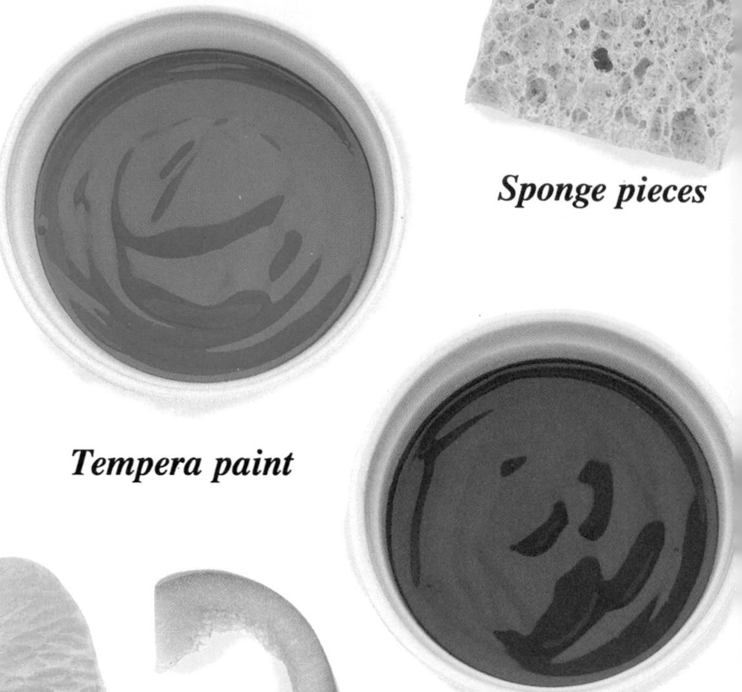

Tempera paint

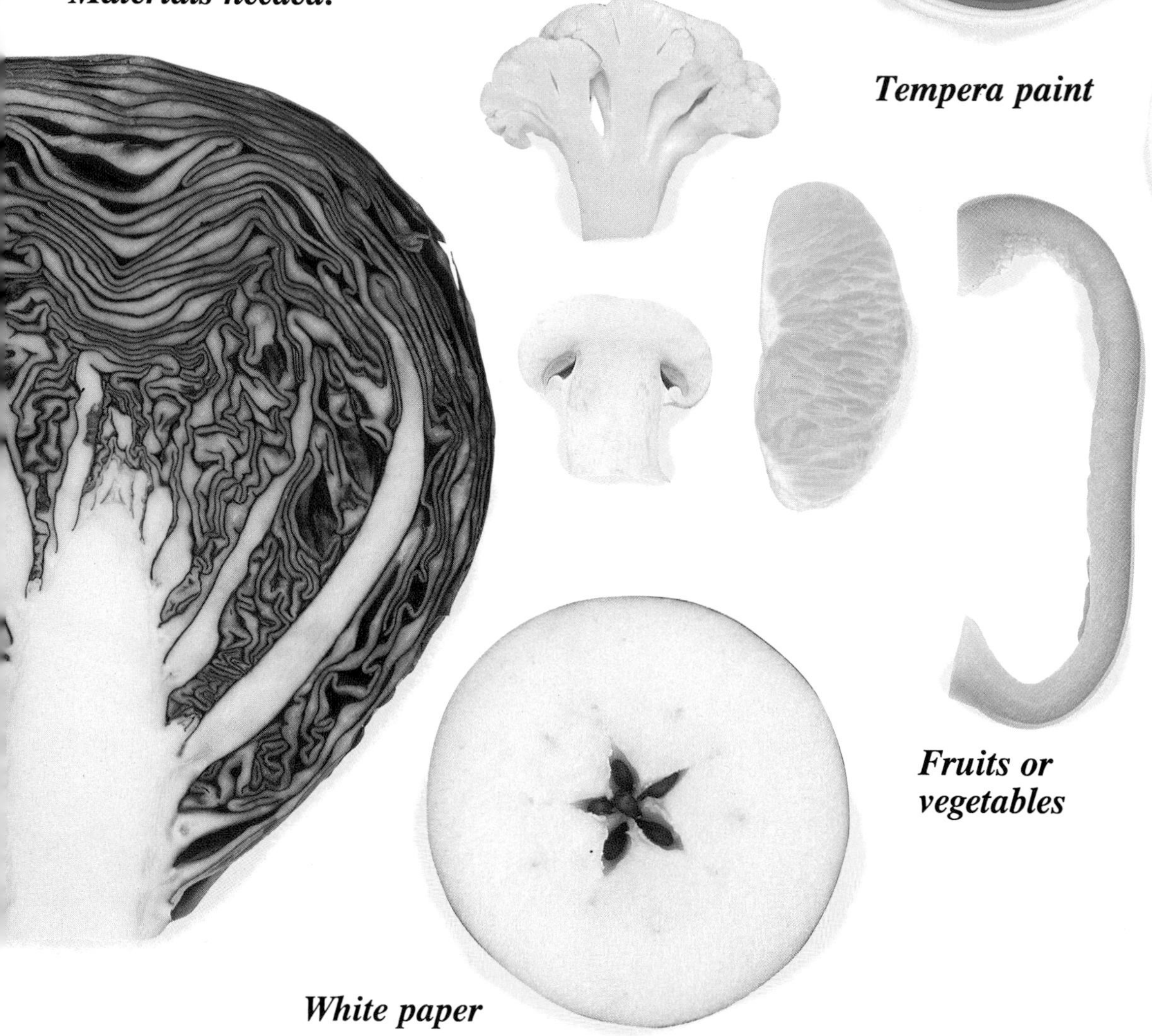

Knife   *Paintbrush*

Fruits or vegetables

White paper

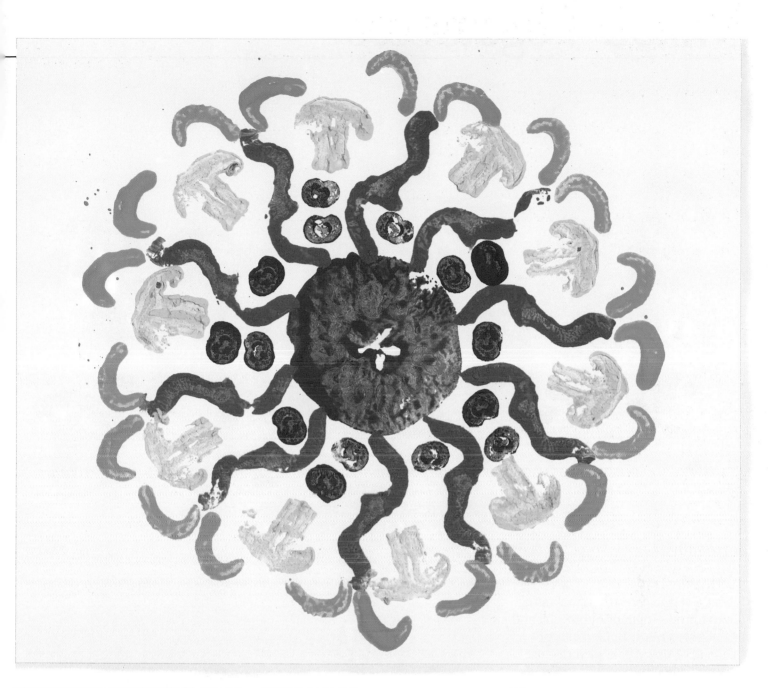

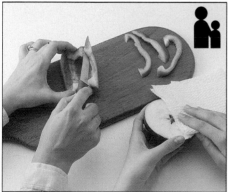

1 Have an adult help you slice each fruit or vegetable smoothly down the middle. Pat it dry with paper towels.

2 Use a paintbrush, sponge pieces or your fingers to cover the sliced surface with paint. Press it onto paper to print.

3 Create a circle design by printing different veggie shapes around the center shape, keeping the pattern the same on each side.

Mixed Vegetables

Print a veggie forest! Draw slanting lines for hills, then print broccoli and cauliflower trees. Build a car, or animal, or any veggie picture—use your imagination!

Make a veggie face, using different vegetables to create eyes, nose, mouth and hair. Or make a beautiful bouquet of flowers.

123

Soap Block Printmaking

Understanding Positive and Negative Images

You can carve interesting designs into flat bars of soap and use them to print dozens of beautiful pictures.

Materials needed:

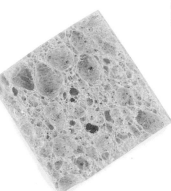

Tempera paint (or water-based printing ink)

Sponge piece (or brayer)

Carrot peeler and masking tape

Carving Your Block

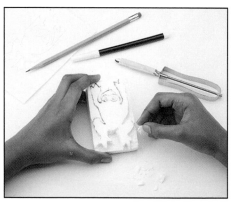

1 Trace the block on a piece of paper and plan a simple design with a pencil. Draw your design on the soap with a felt pen.

2 Use the carrot peeler wrapped with masking tape to carve around your design. Clean off the soap bits and throw them away.

Caution! Always push the carving tool **away** from you. Turn your block when you need to carve in a different direction.

Container for mixing and liquid dish soap

Pencils and a felt-tip pen

Bars of soap

White paper
Scrap paper

Printing Your Block

1 Dip the sponge piece into the paint and pat it onto your carved block. You may need to add a drop of dish soap to the paint.

2 Or, use a brayer to roll on a thin layer of ink. Place the block paint or ink side up on a clean piece of scrap paper.

3 Set a piece of white paper on top, hold it in place, and gently rub with your fingertips. Lift the paper to see your printed design!

Super Soap

These two prints are negative images, where the shapes were cut out of the soap.

Printing with colored paint on white or colored paper gives your picture a special look.

Use your fingertips to dab colored paints on different parts of your block for exciting results!

Positively Negative

The next time you get pictures developed, ask to see the pieces of negative film. You'll see a reverse image of the people and things in the photographs!

Tempera Silk Screens

Making a Silk Screen

Silk screening is a stencil process using fabric. The cloth is specially prepared so that when paint is pushed through, it prints a design onto paper underneath. Silk screen printing is easy when you use a common embroidery hoop and thin cotton cloth.

Tempera paint

Embroidery hoop

2 yards (2 meters) cotton organdy cloth.

Materials needed:

Masking tape

White glue

Pencil

1 To make a hoop screen, cut a piece of cloth a little bigger than the hoop. Take the two rings of the hoop apart and lay the cloth over the bigger hoop.

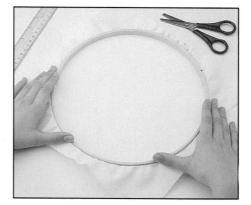

2 Lay the smaller hoop over the cloth and push it down inside the bigger hoop, catching the cloth in between. Pull the edges of the cloth until it's tight like a drum.

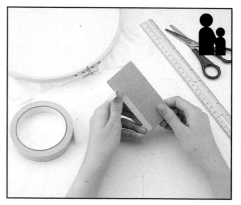

3 Make a squeegee by cutting a 4" by 2" (10 cm by 5 cm) piece of stiff cardboard and wrapping masking tape around one long edge.

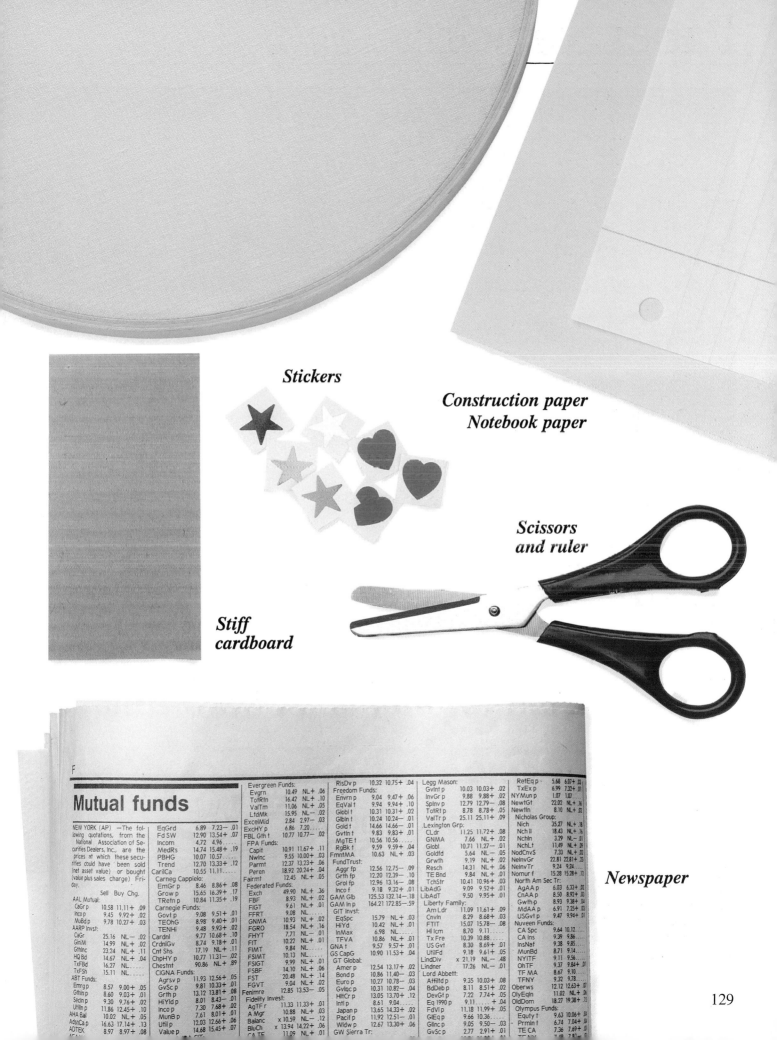

Stickers

Construction paper
Notebook paper

Scissors and ruler

Stiff cardboard

Newspaper

129

Paper Stencils

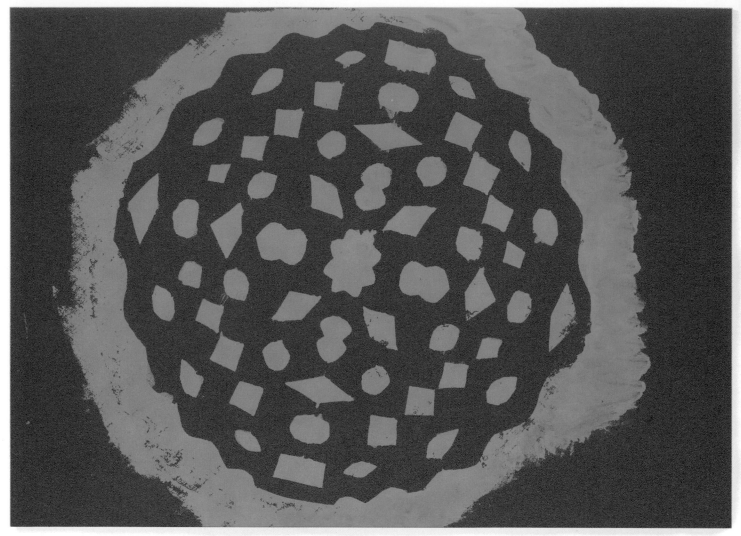

Cut paper design

Cut Paper Stencil

1 Cut a design in a piece of notebook paper. A snowflake works great—fold the paper and cut little shapes out, then unfold it.

2 Lay the cut paper stencil flat on a piece of construction paper. Set your hoop screen down with the stretched cloth pushing down on the stencil.

3 Pour some paint into the hoop. Gently pull the squeegee across the paint three or four times to spread it all over the cloth, scraping extra paint to the side.

Cut paper abstract

Cut paper picture

Sticker abstract

Sticker picture

Sticker Stencil

4 The paint sticks to the stencil and prints a design on the construction paper underneath! Lift the hoop up—paint, stencil and all—and use it again.

5 When you're done, discard the stencil. Take the cloth out of the hoops and wash it in warm water. Use it to print a different cut paper stencil when it's dry.

6 Put a clean piece of cloth in the hoops. Stick pieces of tape and stickers onto the cloth to make a design. Use your squeegee and paint to print onto paper.

131

White Glue Stencil

1 Make a hoop screen and prop it up so the cloth doesn't touch the table. Put scrap newspaper underneath.

2 Draw a simple design or picture on the cloth with a pencil. Squeeze glue onto the cloth along the lines of your pencil sketch.

3 Let the glue dry overnight. Use your squeegee to push paint through the cloth onto construction paper underneath.

132

Part Four: Make Sculptures!

A Note to Grown-Ups

Make Sculptures! features eleven unique sculpting projects plus numerous variations that will fire the imaginations of boys and girls. The projects are open-ended: kids learn techniques they can use to produce sculptures of their own design.

Each project has a theme stated at the very beginning. Children will learn about architecture and design, additive and subtractive sculpture, collage and assemblage, and art forms ranging from clay pots to pop art. They'll use their artistic, fine motor and problem-solving skills to produce beautiful finished sculptures.

But the emphasis of *Make Sculptures!* is on fun. Kids will love experimenting with such diverse mediums as paper, clay, plastic, papier maché, twigs, textiles, plaster and various found objects.

Getting the Most Out of the Projects

While the projects provide clear step-by-step instructions and photographs, children should feel free to substitute and improvise. Some of the projects are easy to do in a short amount of time. Others require more patience and even adult supervision.

The list of materials shown at the beginning of each activity is for the featured project only. Suggested alternatives may require different supplies. Again, children are encouraged to substitute and use whatever materials they have access to (and permission to use!). The projects offer flexibility to make it easy for you and your child to try as many activities as you wish.

Collecting Supplies

All of the projects can be done with household items or inexpensive, easy-to-find supplies. Here are some household items you'll want to make sure you have on hand: newspapers, scrap paper and cloth, cardboard tubes from paper towels or wrapping paper, old hardware and interesting "stuff," plastic cups, plastic utensils, flour, masking tape, duct tape, electrical tape, glue, wire, twine, bucket and sponges.

A Note to Kids

When you build a sculpture, your work isn't flat, like a drawing or painting. It's three-dimensional art—a sculpture goes up and out; it is thick and tall and round. Some sculptures stand on their own. Others hang from the wall. They're all fun to build and look at!

If you want to use a small saw to make Air Towers, a pliers for Funky Junk, or a hot glue gun, get an adult to help you.

Theme Sculptures

Assemblage

Turn your favorite collection into a work of art! Gather seashells at the beach or a box of treasures from around the house. Any group of objects that go together will make a wonderful theme sculpture.

Found objects

Materials needed:

Masking tape

Felt pen

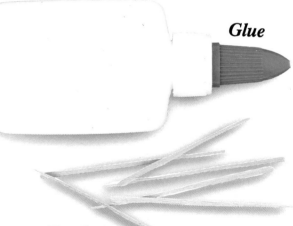

Glue

Plastic or wood base

Toothpicks

1 Pick a couple of large items to go on the bottom. Arrange them so they balance and are sturdy. Use the pen to mark where they touch.

2 Use a toothpick to spread glue over your marks. Put things back together, holding each one in place until the glue starts to dry.

3 Add more little stuff. Use masking tape to hold things in place until the glue dries. You may need several work sessions to finish.

Forest Sculpture

Toy Sculpture

Seashell Sculpture

135

Stuffings

Soft Sculpture

You can make soft sculpture people, animals, toys and pillows—it's easy! Start with cloth or paper. Decorate with paint, crayons or markers. Then staple, sew or glue it together. Stuffing makes your sculpture come to life. You can even sculpt yourself or a friend! (Use big paper like butcher paper or kraft paper.)

Tempera paint

Materials needed:

Glue and clear tape

Marker

Decorations

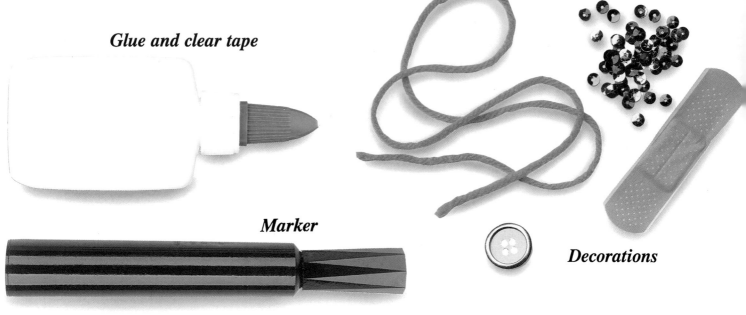

1 Put two layers of big paper on the floor. One person lays down. Another person traces around him.

2 Color the tracing with markers, paint or crayons. Add details to make it look like the real person!

3 Fasten the two sheets of paper together with a few staples. Cut the person out, both layers of paper at once. Save the scraps.

Kraft paper, scrap paper and cloth

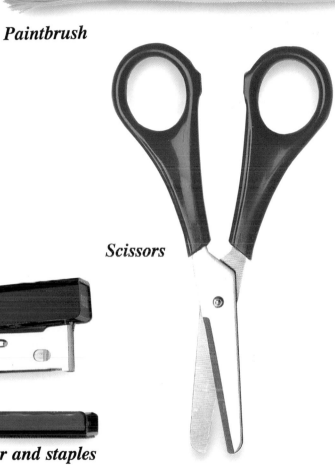

Stick

Paintbrush

Scissors

Stapler and staples

4 Staple around the head—put the staples very close together. Stuff scraps of paper inside. Staple another small area and stuff it.

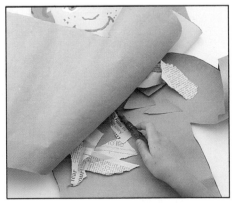

5 Use a stick to stuff paper scraps into hard-to-reach places. Use tape to patch any rips. When it's stuffed full, staple the last opening.

6 Add decorations! Cut yarn for hair, fringe paper for eyelashes, glue on beads, buttons or sequins.

Paper Stuffings

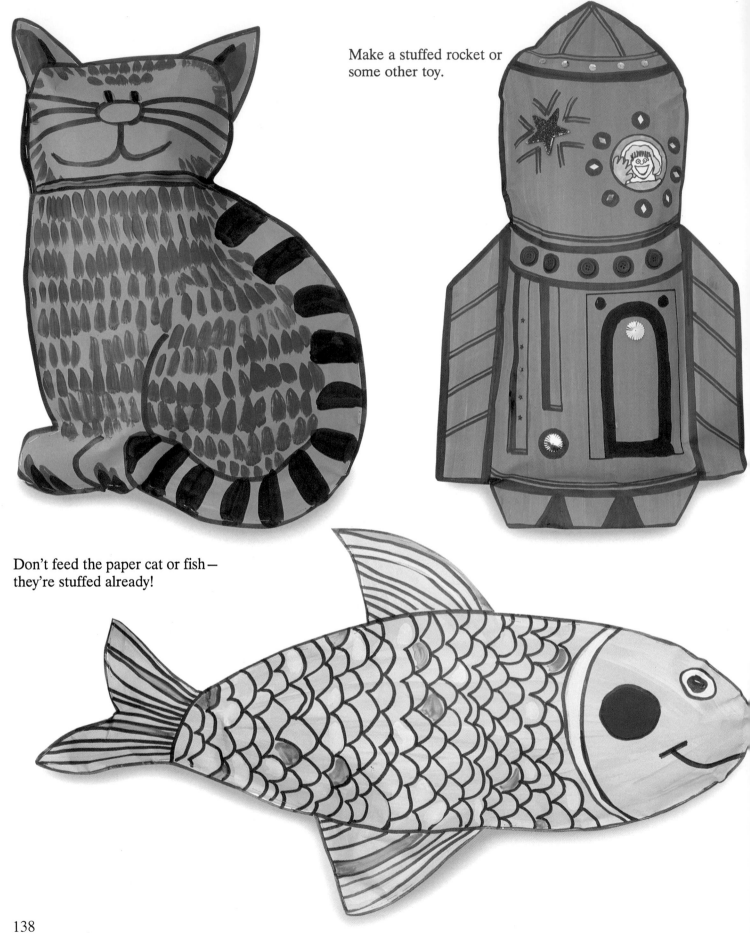

Make a stuffed rocket or some other toy.

Don't feed the paper cat or fish—
they're stuffed already!

These kids have lots of fun decorations. Do you see felt numbers? A real button? A bandage? A necklace? Sequins? Yarn? A real jump rope? A fabric bow?

Fabric Stuffings

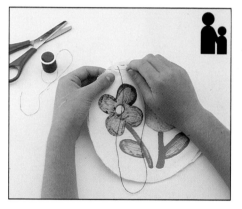

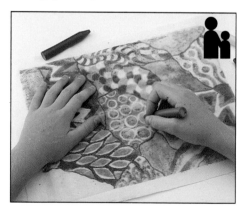

1 Make a soft sculpture pillow! First, draw a design on paper: a circle, square, or simple animal shape will be easy to sew and stuff.

2 Pin two layers of cloth together and cut out the shape you drew. Copy your design onto one of the cut pieces with fabric paint or permanent markers.

3 Put the colored cloth and the other piece together with the colored design facing in. Have an adult help you sew almost all the way around the pillow.

4 Turn the pillow right side out. Stuff it with newspaper or scraps of cloth (or puffy fiberfill from a sewing store for a really comfy pillow).

5 When the pillow is stuffed full, stitch the last bit closed. Be careful with the sharp needle! Ask for help if you need it.

6 You can also draw on the cloth with regular crayons, and have an adult iron your picture between sheets of paper to make the crayon melt into the fabric.

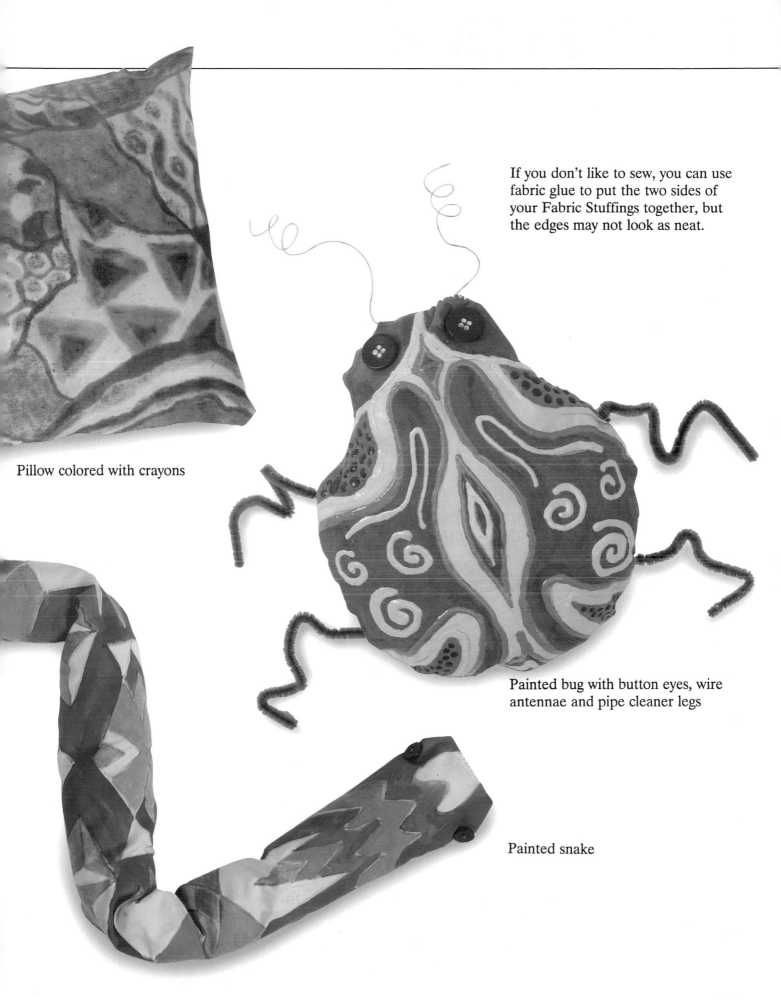

If you don't like to sew, you can use fabric glue to put the two sides of your Fabric Stuffings together, but the edges may not look as neat.

Pillow colored with crayons

Painted bug with button eyes, wire antennae and pipe cleaner legs

Painted snake

Time Capsules

Collage Sculpture

Can you tell a story without using any words? These plastic sculptures let you describe a time or event that is special to you. Use pictures and objects you make and collect, and seal them in a capsule to save forever.

Materials needed:

Scissors

Glue

2 clear plastic cups

Stuff

1 Collect things to tell your story. Clip photos or make things from clay. Arrange them in one of the cups—it will be the bottom cup. Glue them in place if you wish.

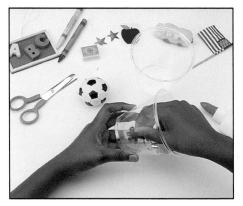

2 To hang something in your capsule, tie or glue it onto a short piece of yarn. Then glue the yarn to the bottom of the other cup—it will be the top.

3 When your arrangement is finished, spread glue all around the rim of the bottom cup. Carefully set the top cup down into the glue to seal them together.

142

*Birthday
Collage*

Baby Collage

*First Day
of School*

Soft Stone Carving

Subtractive Sculpture

Sculptors cut into solid rock with strong tools, carving until the block of stone becomes a beautiful sculpture. When you mix plaster with vermiculite, your block of "stone" will stay soft for a long time—it's easy and fun to carve a sculpture of your own.

When you carve this mixture, use old tools. The plaster would ruin good, metal tools. *Never pour unused plaster down the drain.* Dump it right into the garbage. When you wash it off your hands, use lots and lots of water.

3 scoops vermiculite (see page 6)

Materials needed:

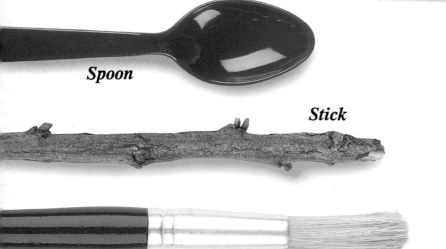

Spoon

Nail

Stick

Paintbrush

Milk carton

1 Measure the vermiculite and plaster into the bucket. Stir it with a stick. Add about two scoops of water and stir until it looks like thick gravy.

2 Pour the plaster into the milk carton. It will turn hard in about fifteen minutes. It will be ready to carve in a half hour.

3 When the half hour is up, peel away the milk carton. Little by little, scrape the plaster with the spoon to shape it. Work over newspaper to catch the scrapings.

Varnish

Bucket and water

Measuring scoop

1/4 CUP 60 ml

2 scoops plaster of Paris

Newspaper

Plastic bag

4 It may take time to get the shape you want. The plaster will stay soft for two or three days if you wrap it in a plastic bag when you stop to rest.

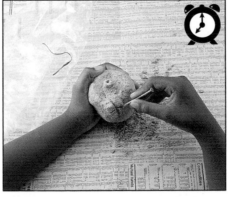

5 Use a nail to carve details into your sculpture. When you're finished, let it dry for two weeks.

6 You can have an adult help you brush varnish on your sculpture when it's completely dry. This will protect it and make it shine.

Soft Stone Sculptures

This sculpture is an *abstract*.

A sculpture of a head and shoulders is called a *bust*.

This apple was made with ground vermiculite mixed with plaster and water. The worm seems to like it!

Your sculpture might look like an ancient figure from far away.

This rabbit was made with flaky vermiculite mixed with plaster and water.

This whale was shaped in a plastic bag and then carved.

Modeling Stone

Another way of sculpting with plaster is to treat it like clay and mold it with your hands before you start to carve.

1 Follow the directions for mixing plaster in Step 1 on page 144. Pour it into a plastic bag. As it starts to harden, squeeze it into the main shape you want for your sculpture.

2 In about a half hour your plaster will be ready to carve. Take it out of the plastic bag and follow Steps 3 through 6 on pages 144 and 145.

Tube Towers

Architectural Sculpture

You'll become a real architect when you make these great tube towers. Learn how to connect tubes and support your tower as you build it higher and higher. Use ribbons, yarn, and colored paper to decorate your sculpture.

Materials needed:

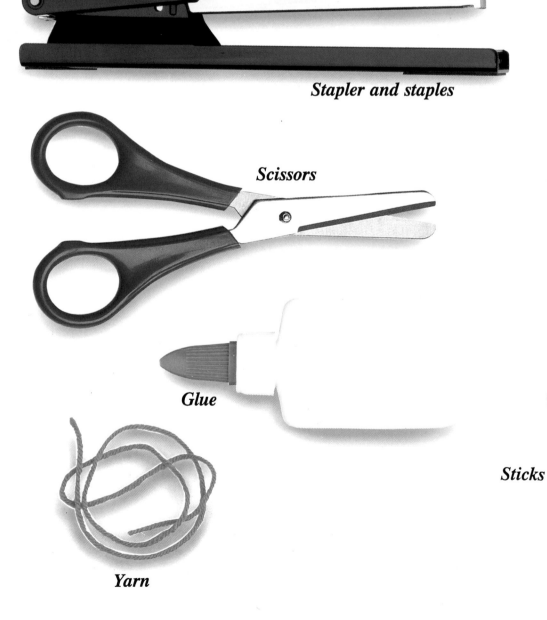

Stapler and staples

Scissors

Glue

Yarn

Sticks

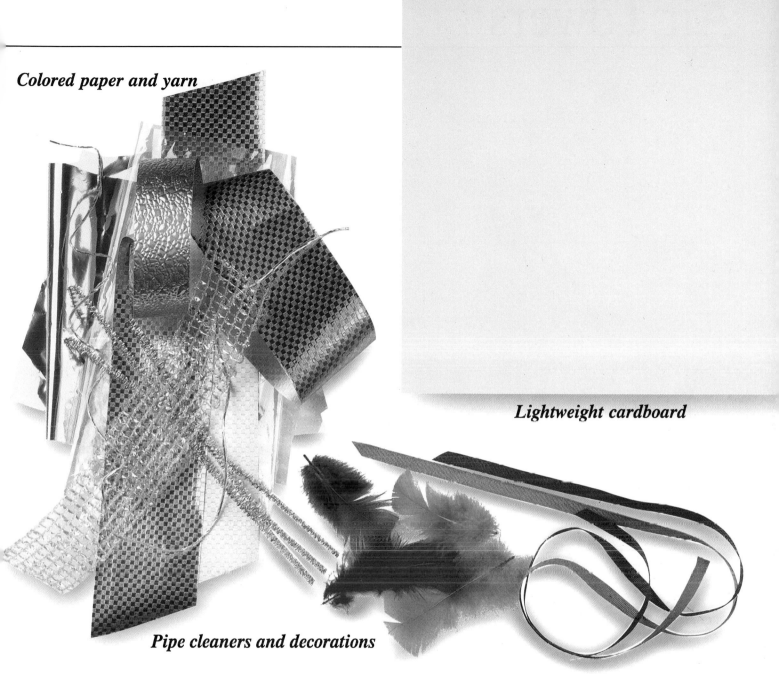

Colored paper and yarn

Lightweight cardboard

Pipe cleaners and decorations

1 Make tubes by rolling cardboard and stapling the ends. Begin putting tubes together with tape or pipe cleaners.

2 Add tubes one at a time. Experiment with ways of putting them together so they'll stand up on their own and be sturdy.

3 When you finish building the tube tower, decorate it with fancy paper, ribbons, yarn and other bright decorations.

Air Towers

The shiny paper used to decorate this structure makes it look like a space station!

This pyramid is made with natural sticks. The yarn and decorations are woven all around. See pages 168 and 169 for another weaving project.

Sometimes it's just too nice to stay indoors. So make an Air Tower outside! Use long sticks or PVC pipes from the hardware store. Connect your tubes with masking tape, duct tape or twine. Work with friends to build your tower higher than your head!

Photo by Fred W. Smith

Fast Food Giants

Pop Art Sculpture

Celebrate your favorite food with a bigger-than-life-size sculpture! Make a pizza slice as big as a poster, or a fabric hot dog to use as a pillow. These fast food giants are more fun than a trip to the ice cream parlor!

Materials needed:

Glue

Fabric glue

Decorations

Scissors

Pizza

1 Design your giant food on paper. Gather paper, fabric, and decorations you can use to make it look real.

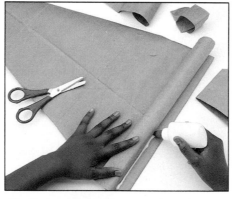

2 Cut a triangle or wedge shape out of cardboard. Cover it with brown paper. Roll up some paper to look like a crust and glue it in place.

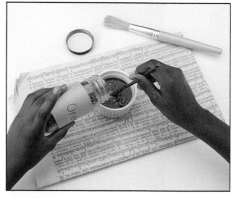

3 Mix real pizza spices or tea leaves with dark red paint to make pizza sauce! Paint it onto your cardboard triangle.

pera paint

**Fabric and
foam scraps**

Colored paper and cardboard

Crayons

Stick

Paintbrush

4 To make pepperoni, splatter white, black, and brown paint on red paper with a stick or toothbrush. Work over newspaper!

5 When the paint dries, cut out big pepperoni circles. Cut other toppings out of paper, too, like green peppers and black olives.

6 This pizza has fabric mushrooms and cheese made of foam. Arrange the toppings and glue them onto the pizza slice.

153

Fast Food Feast

This cheery cherry pie has a crust made of rolled cork (from a craft store). The top crust was cut with a pinking shears. The middle is foam, covered with red fabric and pompons. A sprinkle of red glitter on top looks like cinnamon.

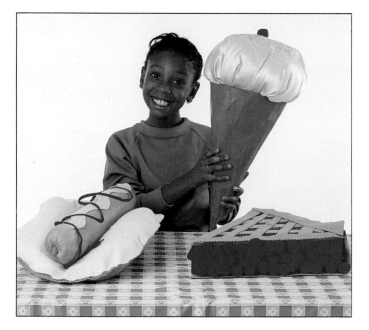

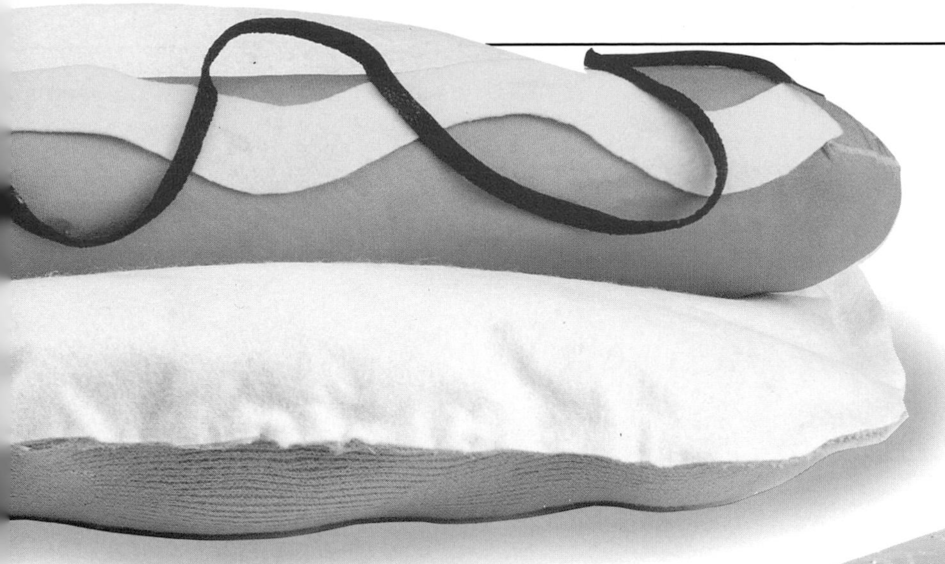

This hot dog is made from foam covered with old pantyhose! The bun is cloth-covered foam, the mustard is felt and the ketchup is a red shoelace.

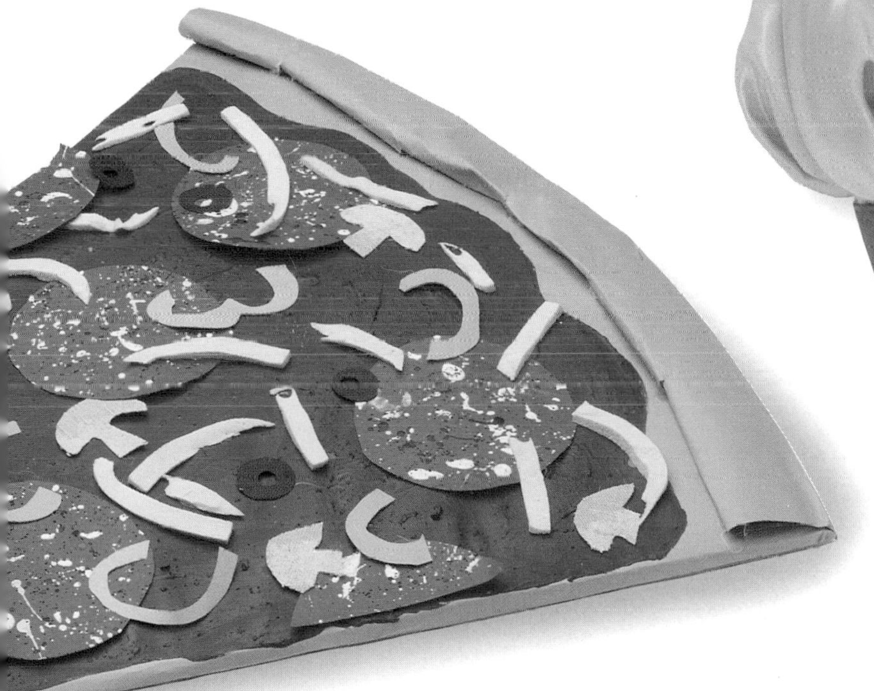

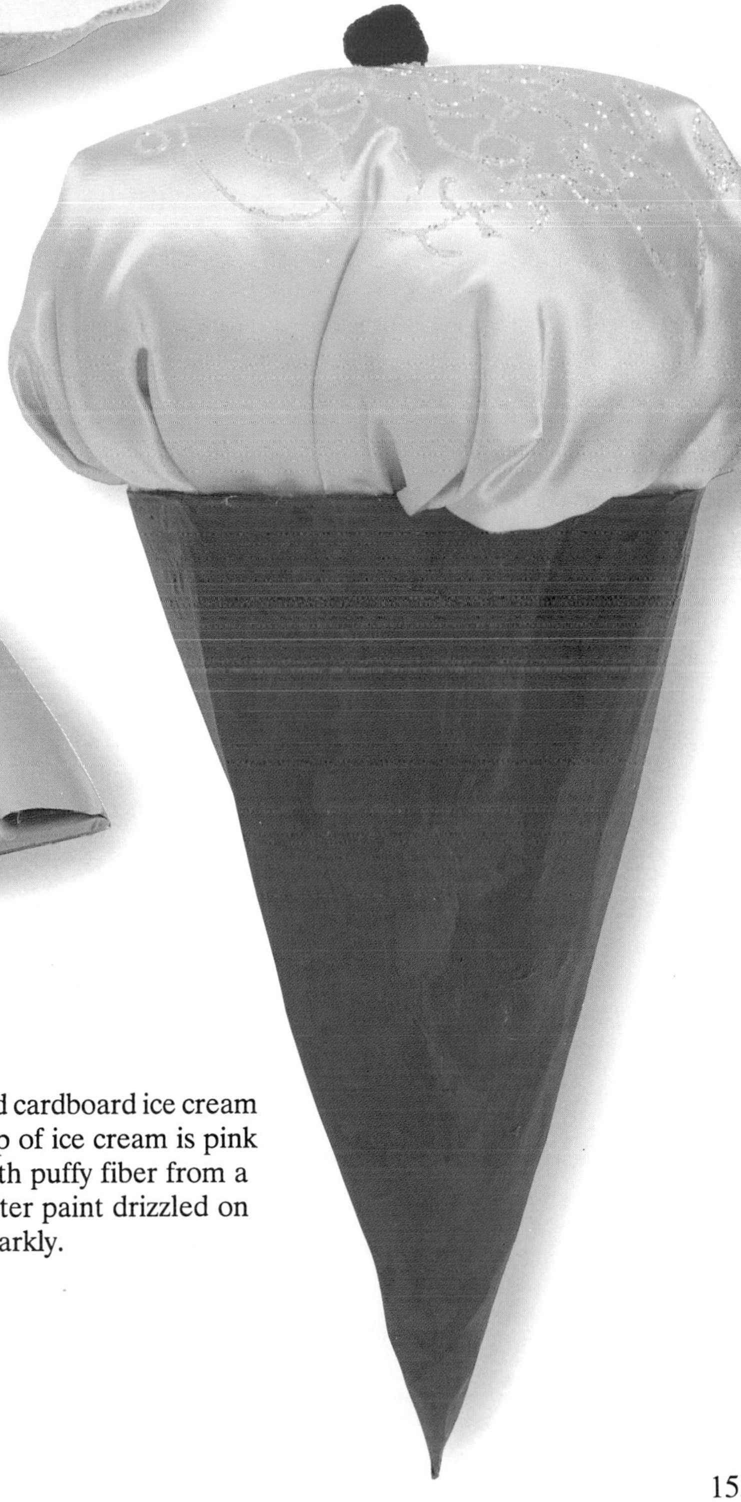

Here's a painted cardboard ice cream cone. The scoop of ice cream is pink satin stuffed with puffy fiber from a craft store. Glitter paint drizzled on top makes it sparkly.

Critter Pots

Sculpting with Clay

It's fun to make little clay pots. It's fun to make statues of animals and birds. But the most fun of all is when you put them together to make critter pots! There are many kinds of clay and dough you can buy at art supply stores or toy stores. Or make your own with this recipe.

Sculpting Dough: Mix 4 cups flour, 1 cup salt, and 1¾ cups warm water in a bowl. Knead with your hands for 10 minutes. Divide up and add different food colors, if you want. Store in a plastic bag when you're not working with it.

Materials needed:

Varnish

Toothpicks

Acrylic paints

Waxed paper

Garlic press

Water

Cheese grater

Dull table knife and a paintbrush

1 Roll an egg-sized piece of clay into a ball. Make a hole in the middle with your thumb.

2 Pinch around and around to make a bowl. The sides of the bowl should be ¼" (1 cm) thick.

3 Now make a critter! Make little balls to shape into heads and eyes. Roll little snakes and pinch them into legs and tails.

4 Cut flat slabs of clay. Trim and pinch them into the shapes of wings or ears.

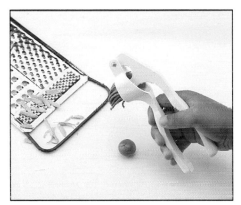

5 Use a garlic press or a cheese grater to make hair or fur, or straw for your animal to eat or sleep on.

6 Join pieces of clay together and rub their edges gently with your finger. Getting your finger wet will help make it smooth.

7 Use toothpicks to carve texture. Add details like teeth, toenails, and nostrils.

8 Let your sculpture air dry for a few days until it's hard. Paint it with acrylic paint — make it look real or silly.

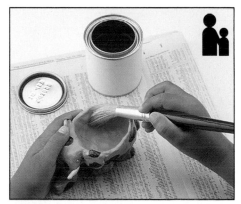

9 Have an adult help you brush on a coat of varnish when the paint is dry. This will make it shiny and will help protect it.

Critter Pots

Elephant Pot

Lion Pot

Panda Pot

Pig Pot

Duck Pot

Frog Pot

Funky Junk

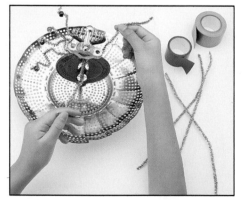

Scissors

Additive Sculpture

Don't throw away that old junk! Be creative
and turn it into original works of art. Invent
new creatures with old machine parts, pieces of
hardware, and used kitchen gadgets. Additive
sculpture is a process of building and adding
pieces as you create. The design is totally up to
you—and your junk!

Materials needed:

Wire

Electrical tape

Carpenter's glue

1 Take a good look at your junk—
do you see a character waiting
to be created? Hold one thing next
to another until you see something
you like.

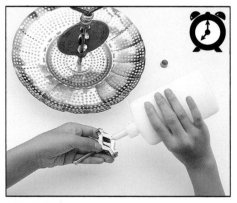

2 When you've found a good
design, begin gluing pieces
together. Build from the bottom up,
working slowly and letting the glue
dry as you go.

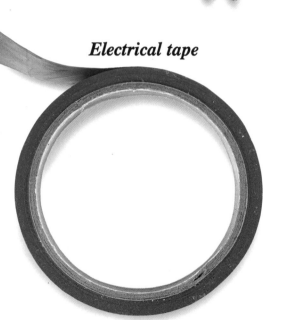

3 Wire or pipe cleaners help hold
things in place. You could also
use duct tape or electrical tape to
hold things together and as part of
your design.

Junk and decorations

Pipe cleaners

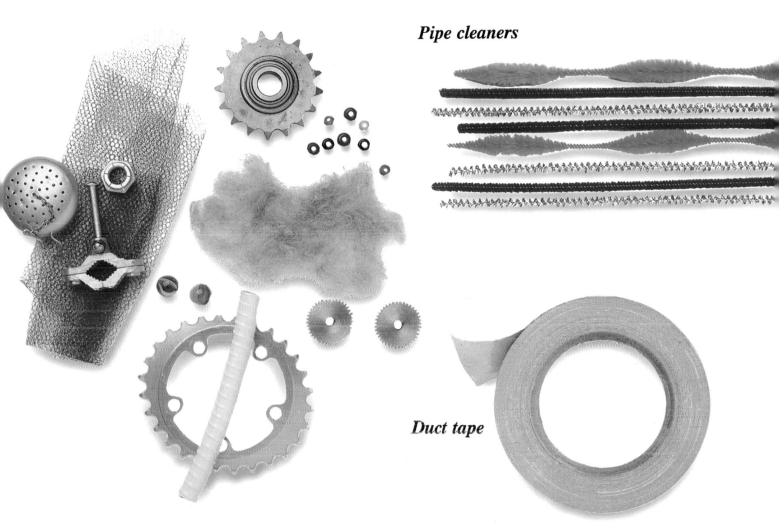

Duct tape

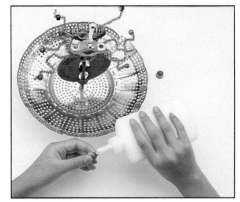

4 Once you've made the basic shape for your character, add decorations to give it life. Glue on wiggly eyes or eyes made of beads or marbles.

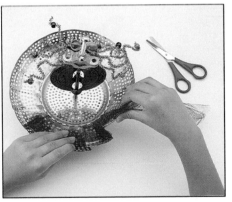

5 Yarn or cotton puffs make great hair. Make clothes out of scraps of cloth or aluminum foil. Bend thin wire to make eyeglasses.

6 Add beads, feathers, and decorations. Cut things out of paper. You decide when your funky junk creature is finished.

Funky Junk

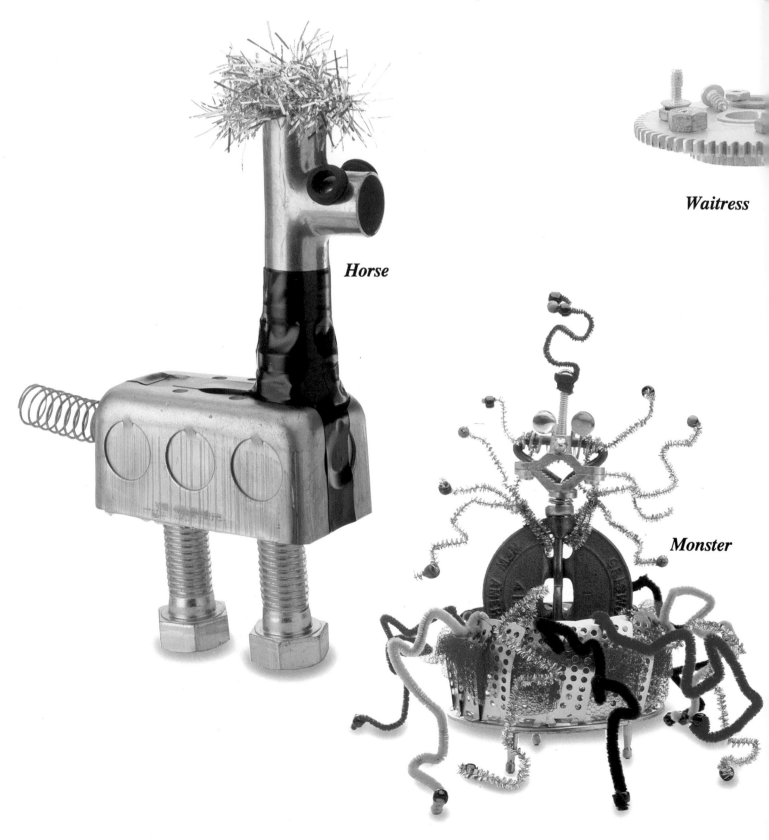

Horse

Waitress

Monster

Lady Robot

Sunflower Guy

Papier Maché Animals

Sculpting with Papier Maché

You can make big, bright sculptures with a simple process called *papier maché*. It's easy, but it takes a long time. You'll need to put on three layers of paper and paste to make it strong. And you have to wait a day in between each layer to let it dry!

Papier maché can be messy—but it doesn't have to be. Wear old clothes and work over newspaper. Throw leftover paste in the garbage, not down the drain. Wipe excess paste off your hands with paper towels before washing them, and use lots of water when you wash.

Bucket

Wallpaper paste or flour and warm water

Newspaper

Materials needed:

Paper tubes

Paintbrush

1 Build the body of an animal. Crumple newspaper and hold it together with masking tape. Use paper plates, boxes and tubes.

2 Use wallpaper paste, or use your hands to mix 2 cups water and 1 cup of flour in the bucket to make a smooth, thick paste.

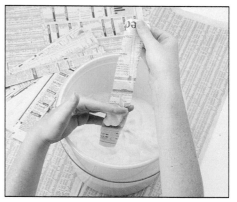

3 Cut or tear newspaper into strips. Dip a strip into the paste and gently pull it through your fingers to rub off extra paste.

Masking tape

Paper towels

Tempera or acrylic paint

Varnish

Small boxes

4 Lay the sticky newspaper strip on the animal frame and smooth it down with your fingers. Use lots of strips and paste to hold the body pieces together.

5 Let the first layer dry overnight. Then add another layer of paper strips and paste. Let it dry overnight. Make a third layer using paper towel strips.

6 Let the third layer dry overnight. Then paint it. Copy a photograph to make your animal look real. Or use bright colors to make a fancy beast.

165

Papier Maché Zoo

Colorful Turtle

When your papier maché animal is dry, have an adult help you spread on a coat of acrylic varnish. This will protect your work and make it shine.

Elephant Calf

Orange Tabby Cat

Silly Reindeer

Your papier maché animals can be small toys or almost life-size decorations for your room, like this baby giraffe.

Wild Alligator

Pinto Horse

Twig Weavings

Textile Art

Everyone knows that you can weave cloth, but have you ever tried to weave sticks? It's easy to turn pretty driftwood or twigs into beautiful wall sculptures with *textiles*: yarn, fabric and soft materials.

Materials needed:

Scissors

Decorations

Twigs

Wire or pipe cleaners

Yarn and cloth scraps

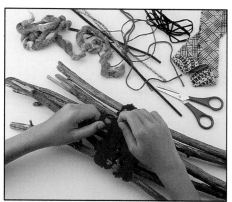

1 Lay your sticks side by side. Twist the pipe cleaners across the middle, going in and out around each stick. Make a loop in the back (for hanging).

2 Cut long pieces of yarn or fabric. Weave with them one at a time. Tie each one to an outside stick and go in and out between the sticks.

3 Push the rows close together as you weave. Each time you get to the end of a cut piece, tie it to an outside stick and trim the end short. Add decorations.

Finished Weaving

Wrap rope and yarn around single
sticks and use them for drumsticks!
Decorate a cardboard oatmeal
container to make a drum.

Fantastic Faces

Paper Sculpture

Masks are made by artists all over the world. People use them in plays, dances, parades and parties. You can make fantastic faces to hang on the wall or make a mask to wear by cutting out eye holes. Staple the face to a paper plate for extra strength (cut eye holes in the paper plate, too!). Make the faces shown here, or design your own.

Materials needed:

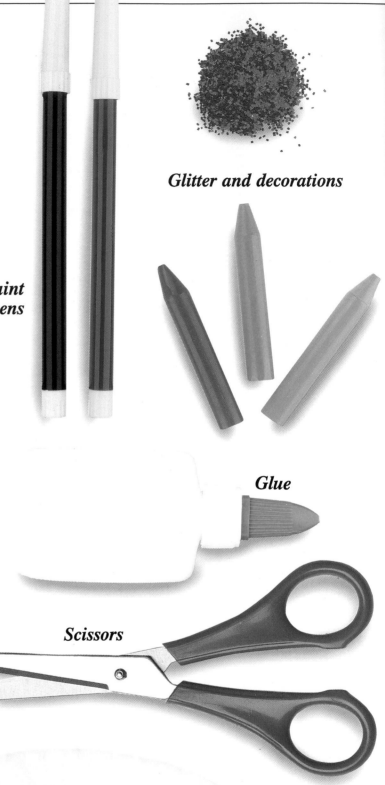

Glitter and decorations

Crayons, paint or felt pens

Colored paper

Foil

Glue

Scissors

Paper plate

Bumps

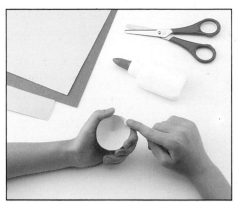

1 Make a circle of paper and then cut into the middle. Spread glue along one edge of the cut.

2 Overlap the other edge of the cut and hold it in place until the glue sets.

3 To glue it onto the face, spread glue along just the bottom of the bump and set it in place.

Nose

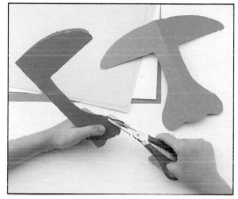

1 Use a bump for an animal nose. For a human nose, fold a scrap of paper in half and cut a shape like the side of a nose.

2 Unfold it and trim until it looks good. You can cut, glue, and overlap the bottom to make it stand up a little.

3 To add eyebrows, fold a scrap of paper in half and cut a shape like this. Unfold and trim it (see the African Mask on the next page).

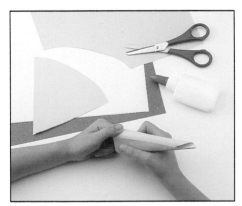

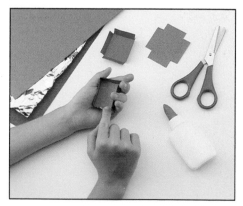

Cone. Cut a wedge of paper and spread glue along one edge. Roll the paper into an ice cream cone shape and hold it until the glue sets.

Curl. Cut a skinny strip of paper and wrap it around a pen. Hold it tight for a minute, then unwrap it and it will stay curly.

Box. Cut a piece of paper into a kind of cross shape as shown. Fold each side up and put glue on the edges (see the Robot Mask on page 173).

Masks and Faces

Twine for hair

Sequins make it sparkle

Little Girl Face

Curls for hair

Cut out the eyes
for a mask

Layers of paper
for decoration

Cut a fringe
for eyelashes

African Mask

Folded paper
cut to look like lace

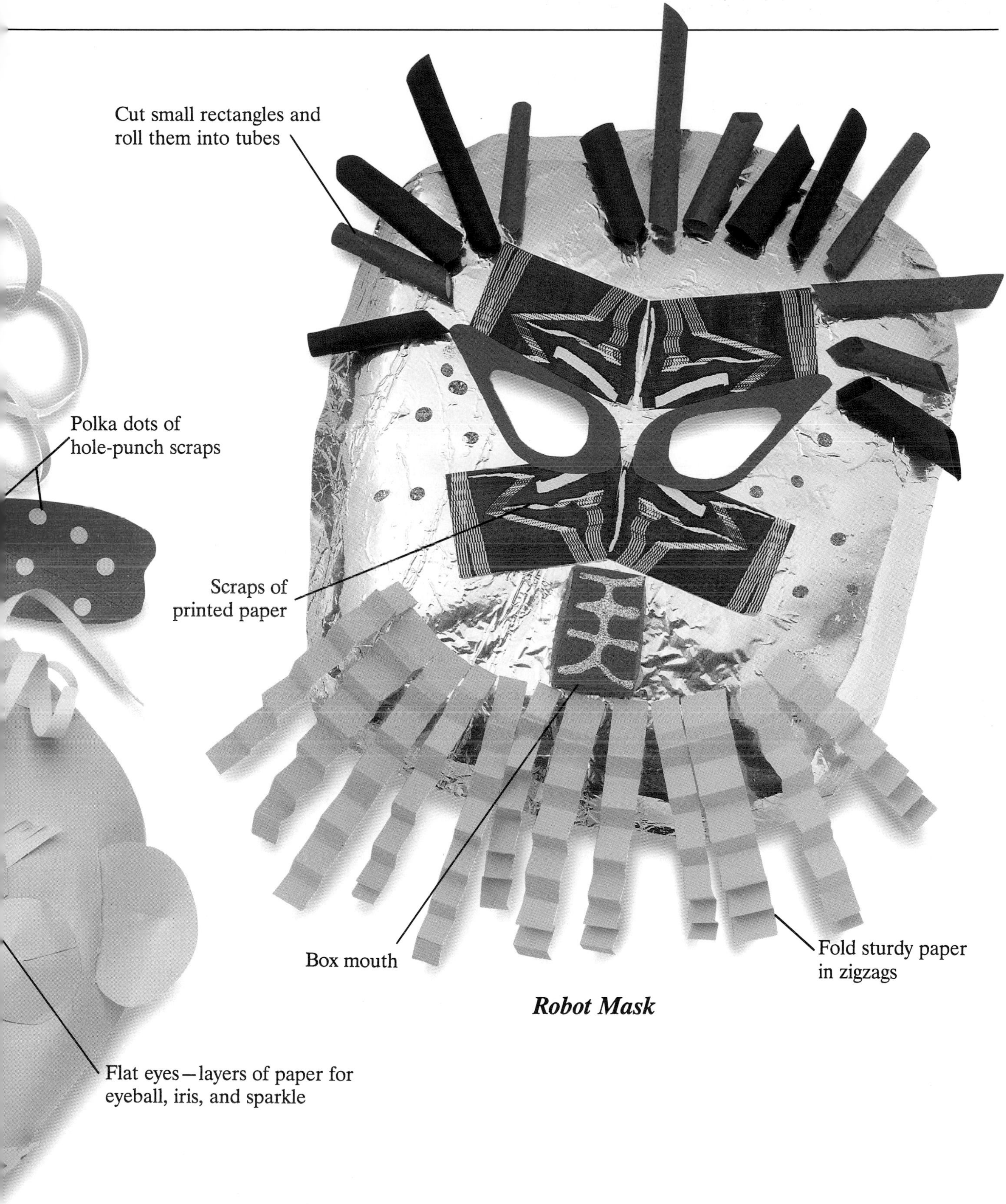

Cut small rectangles and
roll them into tubes

Polka dots of
hole-punch scraps

Scraps of
printed paper

Box mouth

Fold sturdy paper
in zigzags

Robot Mask

Flat eyes—layers of paper for
eyeball, iris, and sparkle

Friendly Faces

Cut slits to fit the ears into the head

Cut a jagged edge for fur

Cut a V up into the bump to make a snout

Bear Cub

Cut a fringe for feathers

Bumps for eyes with a tiny, white triangle sparkle

Cone with the end pinched flat for a beak

Plywood stick for a handle

Bird Face

Part Five: Paint Adventures!

A Note to Grown-Ups

Paint Adventures! features twenty-six unique painting projects. Kids will have fun making bubble prints (blowing bubbles into paint mixed with soap), marbled paper (capturing the design of paint floating on liquid starch), sand paintings, melted crayon paintings, and two-sided op art (where you see one painting from one direction and a completely different painting from the other direction). It's *easy*, and you need only household materials to get started. Wait until you see how much fun your child has whipping up finger paint with soap powder; mixing paint with salt or glue or both; and making his own puffy paint with flour, salt, water and food colors.

By inviting kids to try new things, *Paint Adventures!* encourages individual creativity. The projects provide clear step-by-step instructions and photographs, and examples of finished works; but each project also is open-ended, so kids may decide what *they* want to paint. In addition, *Paint Adventures!* features a lot of ideas for things to make with the finished paintings. So instead of pitching your prodigy's work of art or letting it languish on the refrigerator door, you can make something useful or decorative out of it, or give it as a gift.

Getting the Most Out of the Projects

In the process of doing the art activities, kids learn about pattern, texture, resist painting, encaustic painting, color theory, printmaking and much more. But the kids will enjoy learning because the emphasis is on *fun*.

The list of materials at the beginning of each activity is for the featured project only. Suggested alternatives may require different supplies. Feel free to substitute.

Collecting Supplies

All of the projects can be done with household items or inexpensive, easy-to-find supplies (see pages 5-6 for definitions of art materials you're not already familiar with). Here are some household items you'll want to have on hand: newspapers, paper plates, muffin tins or egg cartons (for holding and mixing paint), margarine tubs (for holding rinse water), drinking straws, cotton swabs, aluminum foil, squeeze bottles (from mustard or dish soap, for example), food colors, plastic bags, shaving cream, white glue, flour, salt, liquid starch, jelly-roll pan, sandpaper and laundry soap powder.

When you see this symbol, look around on the pages of that project for "Helpful Hints." They'll help you get great results.

Bubble Painting

Seeing Patterns

Have you ever blown bubbles and tried to catch them? Try catching colored bubbles on paper! You will see how the shapes and colors repeat. That makes a *pattern*. You can use bubble paintings to color wrapping paper, note cards, lunch bags, book covers and more.

Materials needed:

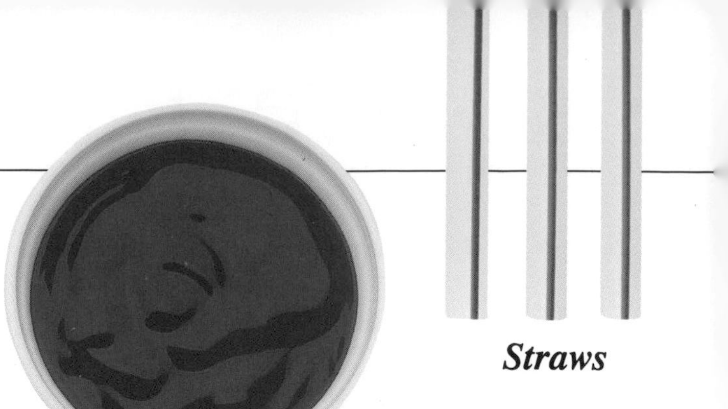

Straws

Small bowl

Tempera paint

Cookie sheet

Dish soap

Paper

Spoon

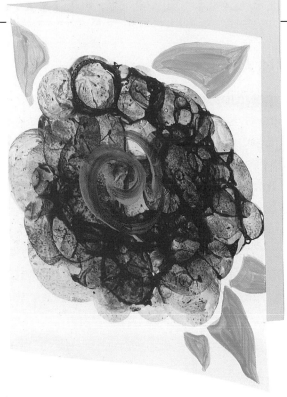

This gift wrap and the note card next to it were made with bubble painting.

Helpful Hints

- If you work with a younger child, *make sure* he knows how to blow through a straw. Sucking in the paint mixture could make him sick.
- If you have trouble blowing good bubbles, add one more spoonful of water.
- If your bubbles are a very light color, add one more spoonful of paint.

1 Put 10 spoonfuls of tempera paint, 1 spoonful of dish soap, and 1 spoonful of water in the bowl. Stir. Put a straw in and blow gently.

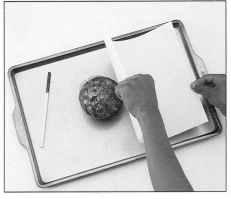

2 When the bubbles rise ½″ to 1″ (2½ cm) above the rim of the bowl, curl a piece of paper and gently touch it to the bubbles.

3 Don't let the paper touch the rim of the bowl. Lift the paper up to see your bubble painting. Let it dry and add another color.

Melted Crayons

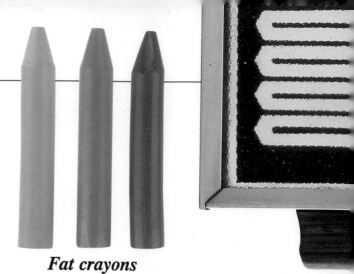

Encaustic Painting

Encaustic painting means painting with wax. Artists used this method in ancient Greece—a long time ago! In this project, you use melted crayons to create paintings rich with color and texture. There are lots of variations to try. You must use heat to melt the crayons, so *ask an adult to help you*. A warming tray works best for safe encaustic painting. If you have permission, you can paint on a cookie sheet, covered with foil, that's been in an oven set at 250°F for ten minutes.

Fat crayons

Materials needed:

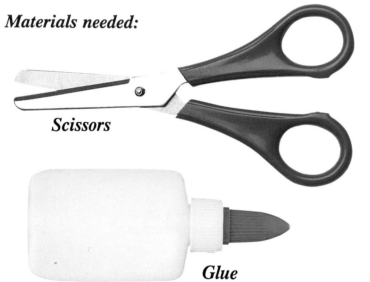

Scissors

Glue

Watercolor paints

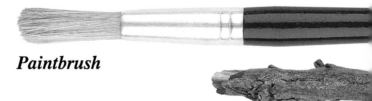

Paintbrush

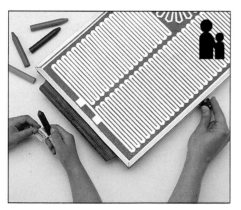

Get Ready. Ask an adult to help you with this project. Set the warming tray to "Low." Peel the paper off of fat crayons.

Draw. Place a piece of paper on the warming tray and draw a picture. Draw slowly so the crayon has a chance to melt.

Comb. Get permission to use an old comb or pick to make interesting lines in your painting.

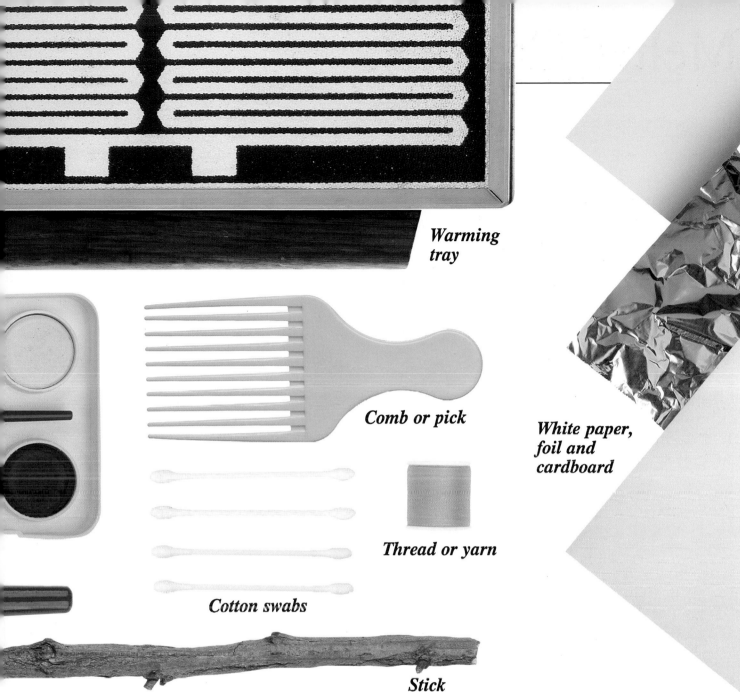

Warming tray

Comb or pick

White paper, foil and cardboard

Thread or yarn

Cotton swabs

Stick

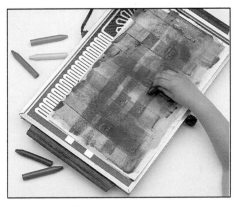

Fat Lines. Use the side of a crayon to paint fat lines. *Be careful* not to touch the tray; it gets hot.

Crumple Foil. Paint a picture or design. Then crumple foil and press it gently into the melted crayon over and over again to make textures.

Cut. When your painting is cool, cut shapes out of it. Hang the shapes from a stick. Or glue them onto another paper to make a collage.

Melted Crayons

Helpful Hint
• If at any time you must hold the paper down against the warming tray, wear an oven mitt or hold a crumpled paper towel to protect your fingers from the heat.

The colorful design below was made more interesting by pressing crumpled foil into the colors while they were still warm.

Above is an encaustic turtle, with texture lines drawn with a comb in the melted crayon.

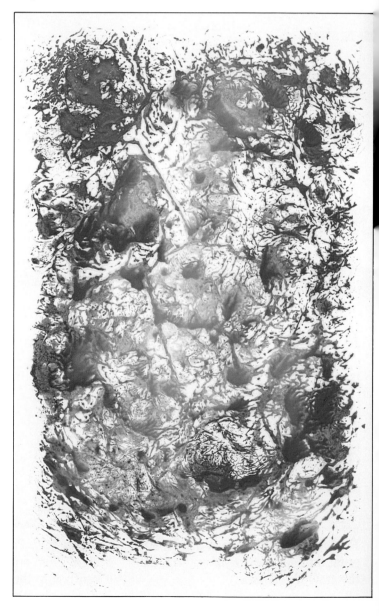

The design to the left is called *plaid*. The wide lines were made by drawing slowly with the sides of the crayons.

Above is a *collage* of shapes cut out of cooled crayon paintings. They look like sea creatures! Blue watercolor paint makes this collage look like an aquarium.

Melted Crayons

The colorful design at left looks like a flower. Here's how to do it: Crumple foil, then uncrumple it and cover the warming tray with it. Then follow the step called "Pull a Print" on page 183.

Above is an encaustic painting done with crayons melted in muffin tins and painted with cotton swabs. It takes a long time to do a thick painting like this, but the results are beautiful!

The bird mobile to the left is made from shapes cut out of a cooled encaustic painting and hung on a stick with yarn. When you hang them in a window, you can almost see through them!

A finished encaustic painting on foil.

Paint on Foil. Cover the warming tray with foil before you turn it on. Wrap the foil around the handles so it won't slip. Draw on the foil.

Pull a Print. Cover the tray with foil and draw a picture. Lay a piece of paper on top and gently rub with a wadded-up paper towel. Lift the paper.

Cotton Swabs. Put crayon bits into a muffin tin on the warming tray, one color in each cup. Let them melt. Paint with short strokes on heavy cardboard.

Tempera Batik

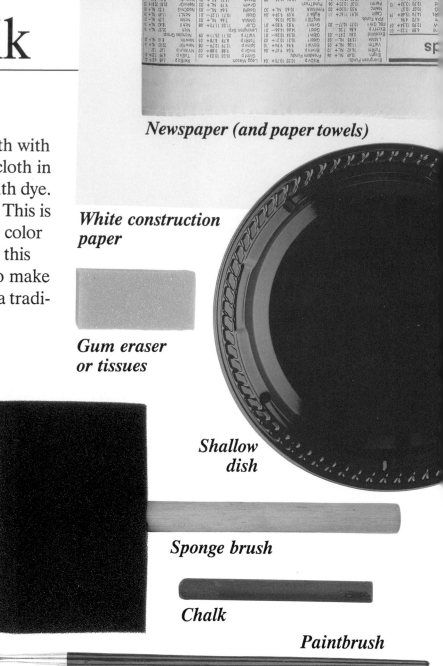

Newspaper (and paper towels)

Learning About Batik

Batik is a way of making designs on cloth with wax and dye. Hot wax is placed on the cloth in some places; then the cloth is colored with dye. Wherever the wax is, it blocks the color. This is called *resist*, because the wax resists the color while the rest of the cloth accepts it. In this project you can use a simpler process to make a resist painting on paper that looks like a traditional batik.

White construction paper

Gum eraser or tissues

Materials needed:

Tempera paint

Shallow dish

Sponge brush

Waterproof India ink

Chalk

Paintbrush

1 Draw a chalk picture on construction paper. Use thick chalk lines. Make the shapes of your drawing large and simple.

2 Paint inside the chalk lines. Use any color but black. Don't paint over the chalk lines. Leave spaces between the colors.

3 Let the painting dry completely. When it's dry, use a gum eraser or tissues to gently wipe away the chalk lines.

184

A finished tempera batik painting.

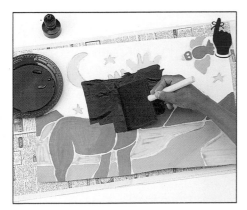

4 Pour ink into a shallow dish. Use a sponge brush to gently cover the painting with *one* coat of ink. Don't overlap brushstrokes.

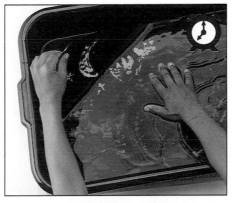

5 Let the ink dry for thirty minutes. Then hold the painting under cool water and gently rub away the ink.

6 Set your painting on newspaper to dry. Here's how it will look. The ink sticks to the painting in some places, just like a batik!

Batik Masks and More

Here's a tempera batik that was used as a book cover. Heavy paper pages were tied together with yarn to make a scrapbook.

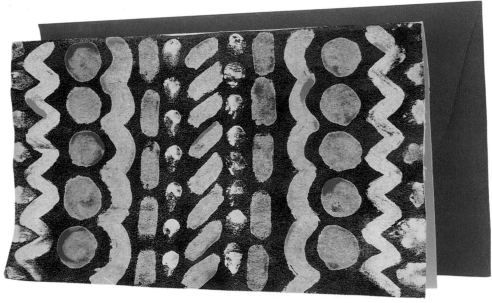

Here's a tempera batik folded in half to make a special card.

Make a Mask

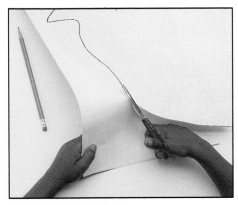

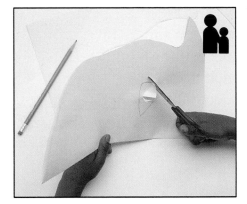

1 Fold a big piece of construction paper in half lengthwise. Draw a curvy, twisting line. Cut along the line; don't cut along the fold.

2 Have an adult help you figure out where the eyes should go. With the paper folded, cut eye holes out of both layers at the same time.

3 Now unfold the mask and batik it, using steps 1 to 6 on pages 184 and 185. Decorate it with feathers, yarn, glitter or sequins if you wish.

When your mask is dry, punch holes on each side and tie yarn at each hole. Tie the yarn behind your head to wear your mask. Don't wear it outside if you can't see well through the eye holes.

Helpful Hints

- When you wash your paintbrush between colors, dry it with paper towels. It's important for the paint not to be watery.
- *Washable* tempera paint isn't good for this project. It will wash away when you rinse off the ink.
- Only hold your painting under water until the picture appears. Some black will remain. If you soak it too long, you will damage the paper.
- It might help to support your paper on a cookie sheet or board while rinsing.

Puffy Paint

Making and Using Textured Paint

Paintings aren't always flat. With common supplies from your kitchen, you can make your own paint that's puffy! Use it to add thick lines to your other paintings. Or use it to decorate boxes, frames, light switch covers and more.

**Mixing bowl
and flour, salt and water**

Materials needed:

Paintbrush

Pencil

Food coloring

Scissors

**Glue and
acrylic varnish**

**Spoon and
small dishes**

Squeeze bottles

Papers

A finished puffy painting.

1 Mix 1 cup flour, 1 cup water and 1 cup salt. Divide it into several dishes. Add food coloring to make a different color in each dish.

2 If you have several bottles, fill each one with a different color. Then pick up whichever bottle you need and add puffy colors to your painting.

3 If you have only one bottle, squeeze one color in all the places you want that color to be. Then wash the bottle and use it to paint the other colors, one at a time.

Puffy Stuff

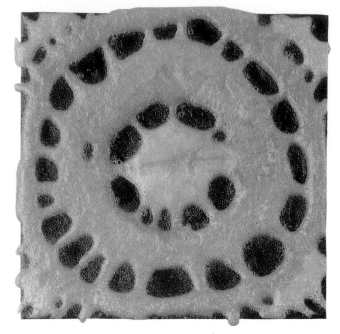

Above is a finished puffy paint box for storing jewelry.

Below is a heart-shaped puffy paint box that would make a great gift filled with candy or little surprises.

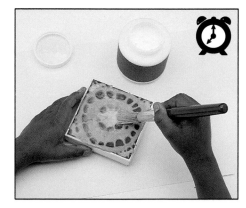

Cover a Box

1 Trace around the bottom of the box on colored paper. Cut out the shape you draw.

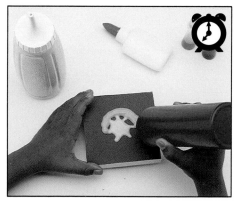

2 Glue the cut paper to the top of the box. Paint a puffy design following steps 1 to 3 on page 189. Let it dry overnight.

3 Brush on a coat of acrylic varnish to protect your work and make it shine. Let it dry overnight.

Above is a matboard frame. You can buy matboard at framing stores or art supply or craft stores. Matboard is cut to fit inside of store-bought frames. But if you color a piece with puffy paint, it becomes a beautiful frame all by itself.

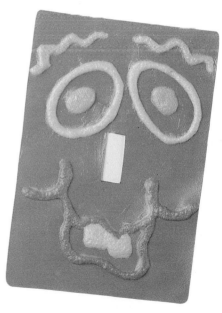

Get permission to make a cover out of heavy paper for your light switch plate. Color it with puffy paint to jazz up your room.

The Color Wheel

Color Theory and Experiments

Red, yellow and blue are called *primary* colors. When you mix one primary color with another primary color, you get a *secondary* color. The secondary colors are green, orange, and violet or purple.

In a rainbow, the primary and secondary colors always appear in this order: violet, blue, green, yellow, orange, red. The colors on the color wheel are arranged the same way.

Here's a color wheel with pictures of natural objects that are primary and secondary colors. On the next page are some color experiments to try.

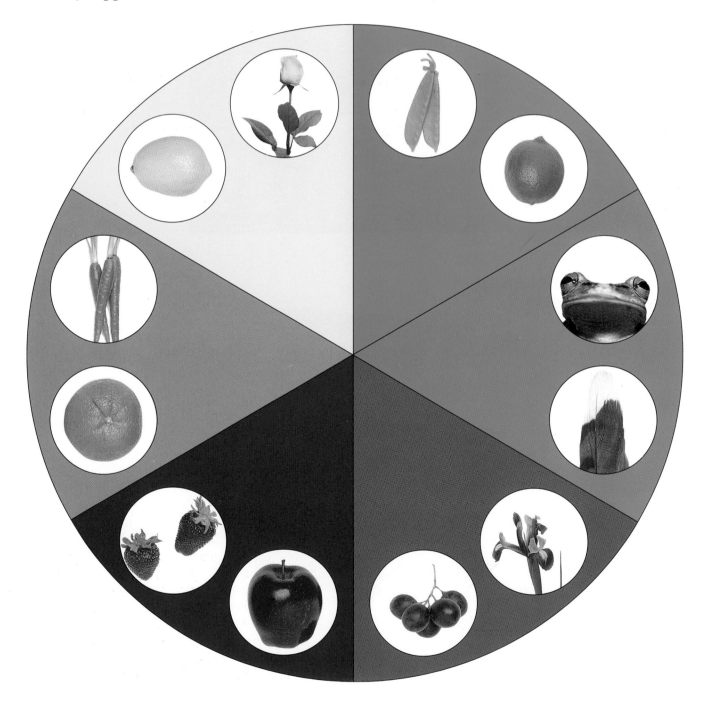

Fill a jar with water. Add food coloring one drop at a time and watch the colors slowly blend to make new colors. Try these combinations:

- 1 drop of red + 3 drops of yellow
- 2 to 4 drops of yellow + 2 drops of blue
- 3 to 4 drops of red + 2 drops of blue

Squirt some foamy shaving cream into a clear plastic bag. Drop food coloring on the sides — one primary color on each side. Seal the bag and squish the shaving cream until the colors mix. Now what color do you see?

Spinners. Put a cup on heavy white paper or thin cardboard. Trace around it and cut out the circle. Draw three lines that cross in the center to make six even wedges. Paint every other wedge red. Let it dry. Paint the other wedges either blue or yellow. Push a toothpick through the center. Now spin it like a top. What color do you see? Your eyes will be fooled!

Color Power

Mixing Colors

On pages 192 and 193, you can learn about the color wheel. Here is a project to try *using* the color wheel. By mixing the primary colors (red, blue, yellow) you can make the secondary colors (green, orange, violet) and use them in a painting.

Materials needed:

White paper

Paintbrushes

Rinse water

Paper plates

Tempera paint: red, blue, yellow

Pencil

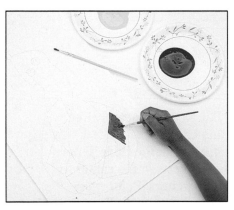

1 Draw a picture that has six of the same shapes, like the diamonds on this snake's back. Paint the first shape red.

2 On a plate, add yellow paint to red and mix it. The color should be orange. Paint the next shape with the orange paint.

3 Paint the third shape with the yellow paint.

Helpful Hint
• Use a different paintbrush for each color of paint, or rinse your brush thoroughly each time you change colors.

4 Add some blue paint to yellow and mix it. The color should be green. Paint the next shape green.

5 Paint the fifth shape with the blue paint.

6 Add some red paint to the blue and mix it to make violet, or purple. Paint the last shape purple. Then paint the rest of the picture.

Op Art

Optical Art

In the 1960s, some artists made paintings with geometric shapes that they called *op art*. These paintings were like optical illusions because they tricked people who looked at them. Sometimes the shapes and colors appeared to be moving! Or a viewer might see one painting from one direction, and a different painting from the other direction. (There's an op art project like that on pages 198 and 199.)

Here is a three-dimensional op art project that uses tints. *Tints* are made by adding more or less of a color to white, making it look darker or lighter. You'll see!

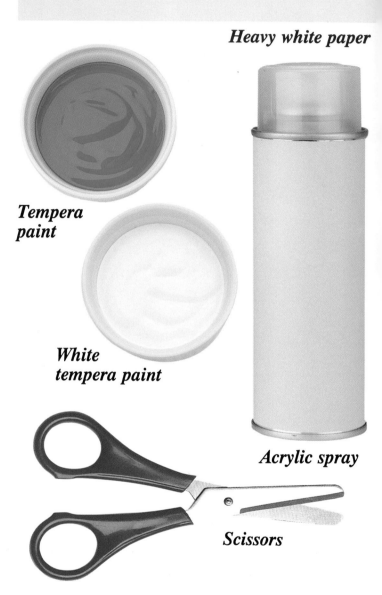

Heavy white paper

Tempera paint

White tempera paint

Acrylic spray

Scissors

Materials needed:

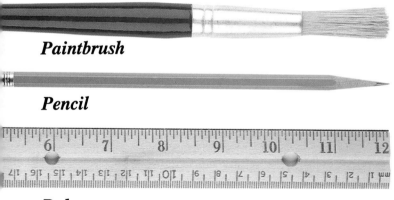

Paintbrush

Pencil

Ruler

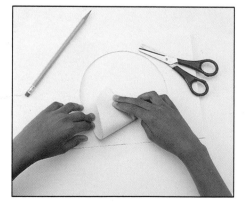

1 Draw a circle, square, oval or diamond on a piece of white paper. Cut it out. Fold the shape in half and then in half again.

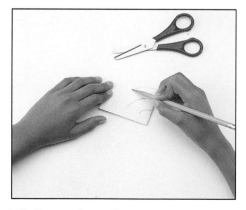

2 Draw three lines from the side that is one folded edge toward the side that is two folded edges. Don't draw all the way to the end.

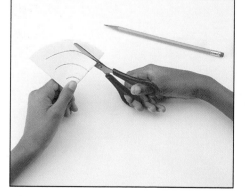

3 Cut along the lines you drew. Don't cut all the way to the end. Stop where your drawn lines stop. Unfold the shape.

When your hanging is dry, fold half of the center shape toward you and the other half away from you. Then fold the two halves of the ring next to the center the opposite way. Fold the next ring the same way you folded the center. Fold the outside ring the same direction you folded the one next to the center. Use a needle to poke thread or yarn through your op art so you can hang it up.

4 Make a very light tint by mixing a little color with white. Paint the outside ring with it. Let it dry. Paint the other side of that ring.

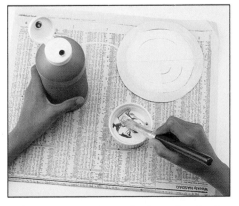

5 Make another, darker tint by adding a bit more color to the first tint. Paint the next ring on both sides with this darker tint.

6 Make the last tint, darker still, and use it to paint the third ring. Paint the middle with the pure color—not mixed with white at all.

Op Art

If you were to look at your op art unfolded, it would not look like a painting at all. But fold it, and—magic! Walk by it from one direction and see one painting; walk by it from the other direction and see the other painting!

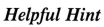

Helpful Hint
- You may want to use opposite ideas for your paintings such as day and night, winter and summer, or land and sea.

1 Make two paintings, each on a piece of paper 9″ by 12″ (size A4). For true op art, the paintings should be very different.

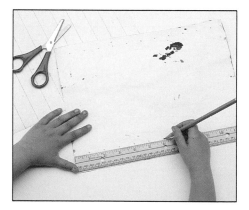

2 When your paintings are dry, turn them over. Make marks 1″ (2½ cm) apart along the top and bottom. Connect the marks with lines to make strips.

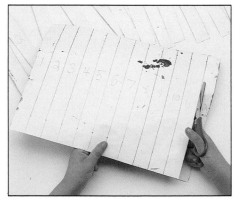

3 Number each strip, left to right, from 1 to 12. Do this on both paintings. Cut the strips apart.

4 Glue the strips onto a piece of heavy paper 9″ (23 cm) by 24″ (61 cm). First do 1 from the first painting, then 1 from the other painting. Then 2 and 2, and so on.

5 Fold the heavy paper like an accordion, using the strips as guidelines for folding. You can make each fold over a table edge to get straight lines.

6 Have an adult help you spray the op art with hairspray or clear acrylic.

Marbled Paper

Marbling

Marbling is a way of coloring paper to look like a type of stone called marble. Touch paper to paint floating on liquid. When you lift up the paper, you will see beautiful swirls of color.

It's fun to make lots of marbled paper, trying different colors and different swirly patterns. Then, have even more fun *making* things with your marbled paper. See pages 201 to 203 for ideas.

Materials needed:

Cookie sheet

Liquid starch

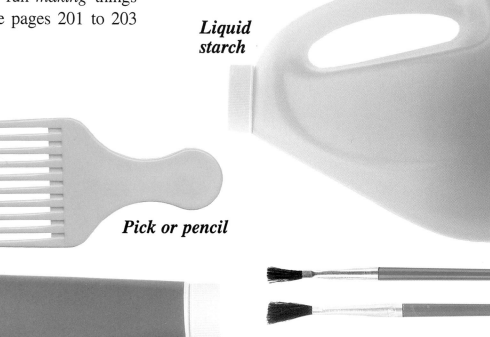

Paper

Pick or pencil

Acrylic paint

Paintbrushes

1 Pour liquid starch on the cookie sheet, about ¼″ (½ cm) deep. Carefully drop watery acrylic paint (2 to 3 teaspoons water to 1 teaspoon paint) onto the starch.

2 Use the pick or a pencil to make swirls in the colors. Work quickly! The paint will sink into the starch, so you must capture the color while it's still floating.

3 Curl a piece of paper. Touch the center to the liquid and gently let go of the edges. The paper should sit on the liquid.

Touch a white lunch bag to the swirled paint and make a beautiful gift bag! Marble a piece of paper with the same colors and cut it to make a matching card. This one has a piece of ribbon glued on.

Helpful Hints

- If the paint sinks into the starch right away, you need to mix more water with the paint before dropping it onto the starch.
- It takes a lot of starch to make even a thin layer on the cookie sheet shown here. To save on starch, use a smaller pan and smaller pieces of paper.

4 Gently lift the paper up, starting at one side. The swirls of color will now be on the paper.

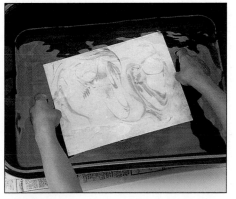

5 Rinse the paper to remove the starchy film. It will take only a few seconds. Don't rinse it longer than that or the paint will come off.

6 Let the marbled paper dry on newspaper. Drip more watery paint onto the starch and you can make another piece of marbled paper.

Marbled Paper Products

Create a matching desk set by covering a can to make a pencil holder, and a small box to hold paper clips, rubber bands or little treasures.

Make your own book with a marbled paper cover. Cut the cover and all the pages the same size. Make two holes with a hole punch and tie it all together with a ribbon.

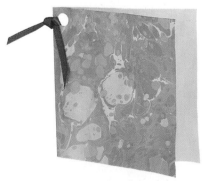

Making Combs

Create your own comb or rake! Make a comb by pushing straight pins through a stick of balsa wood. It is very important that the pins be evenly spaced; these are about ½ cm (less than ¼ inch) apart. Be careful with this sharp tool!

A rake is made of toothpicks taped to heavy cardboard. They are spaced farther apart—about 2 cm (¾ of an inch) between each one.

Experiment dragging these tools up and down and back and forth through the drops of paint floating on the starch. See what designs you can make. Here are a few examples of traditional marbling patterns.

Don't overdo it! For each sheet of marbled paper, only comb or rake through the colors two or three times. Otherwise the colors will run together and look muddy.

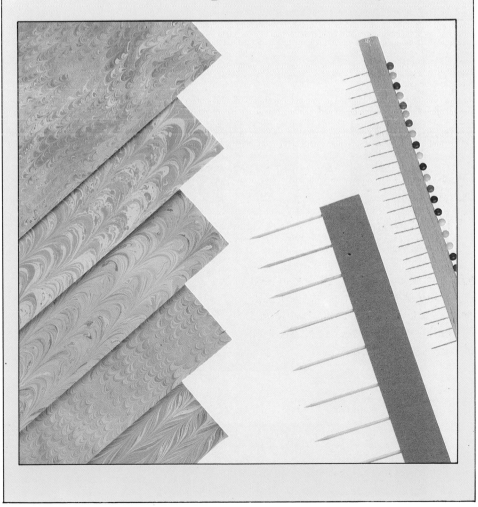

Cut a long, thin bookmark and tie a ribbon through a hole punched at the top. Or make a small gift card.

Scrap Magic

Fun Things to Make

What do you do with your paintings when you're finished painting them? You can make beautiful weavings with two paintings that are the same size (you can cut them to make them the same size if you need to). Or, if you've cut up some of your paintings to make note cards, bookmarks or collages, use the scraps to make paper quilts.

Quilts have been made in America since colonial days. Traditional quilts are sewn with scraps of material. You can make paper quilt squares with scraps of cut paintings. This quilt has pieces of a melted crayon painting, a bubble painting and marbled paper. Cut geometric shapes and arrange them in a pattern on a piece of construction paper. When you make a pattern you like, glue the pieces in place.

This is two salt paintings woven together. See instructions for making a salt painting on page 211.

1 Cut slits into one painting. Don't cut all the way to the ends.

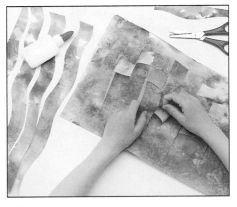

2 Cut the other painting into straight, wavy, or zigzag strips. Weave them over and under the slits in the other painting.

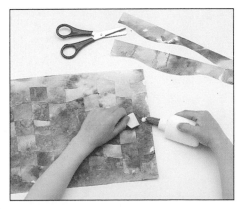

3 Glue the ends of the strips to the top and bottom edges of the slit painting.

Sand Painting

Navajo Sand Painting

Many years ago the Navajo Indians created paintings in the sand. They colored the sand with powder made from ground-up rocks. The paintings were created for special ceremonies and then destroyed after the ceremony was over. It's easy and fun to make your own sand paintings using sandpaper, glue and colored sand. Imitate traditional Indian symbols or create your own symbols using lines, colors and shapes.

Colored sand from a craft store

Materials needed:

Feathers and decorations

Dish for mixing 1 tablespoon water with 1 tablespoon glue

1 Draw a design on the sandpaper with a pencil. Choose the colors of sand you want for your design and place them on separate plates.

2 Put the sandpaper on the cookie sheet. Brush the watery glue onto all the sections of your design where the lightest color will be.

3 Use a spoon to sprinkle the lightest color of sand onto the glued sections of your design. Sprinkle on a lot of sand.

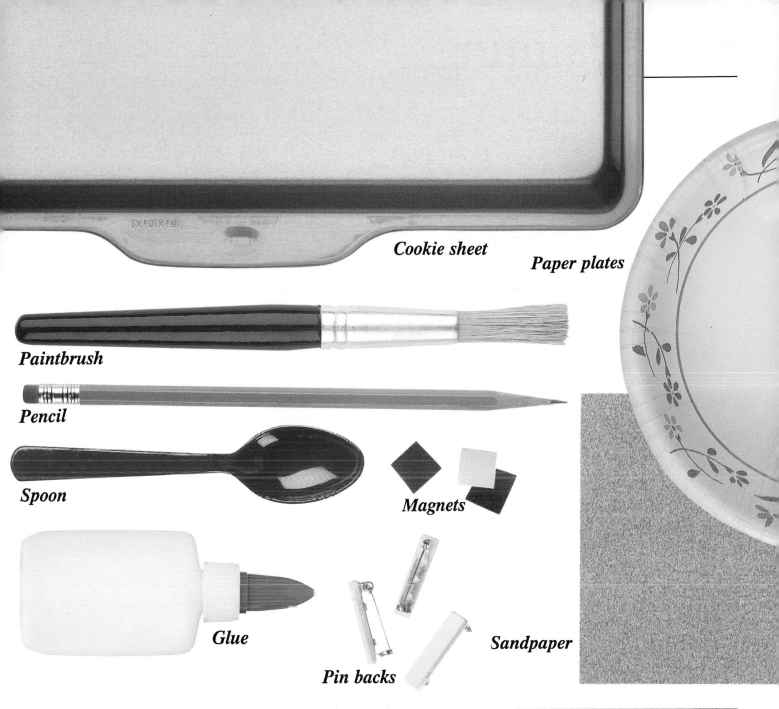

Cookie sheet

Paper plates

Paintbrush

Pencil

Spoon

Magnets

Glue

Pin backs

Sandpaper

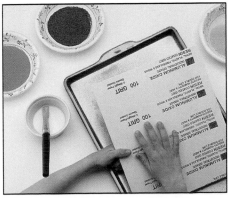

4 Turn the sandpaper over and tap it gently. The loose sand will fall back onto the cookie sheet.

5 Set the painting aside to dry for ten minutes. Carefully pour the sand back onto the paper plate.

6 Now do the next color. Brush on glue, sprinkle sand, tap the back, set it aside to dry. Do all the colors this way.

Sand Painting

Here is an eagle sand painting. The eagle is a traditional Indian symbol. The finished painting was glued to construction paper.

Here is an *abstract* design—it is not meant to look like anything real. It has feathers for decoration! The sandpaper was cut in a circle before painting.

You can cut the sandpaper into little shapes and paint them. Have an adult help you spray them with hairspray or clear acrylic. Then stick magnets or pin backs to the back of them.

Try using colored rice instead of sand. Have an adult help you mix ¼ cup of rubbing alcohol with a few drops of food coloring. Soak the rice for ten minutes, drain it, and set it on waxed paper to dry.

For a natural look, color your own sand by mixing plain, fine sand with cornmeal, ground charcoal, and spices such as cumin, paprika or curry.

Paint Plus

Creating Textures in Paint

Anyone can paint with paint, but have you ever tried painting with paint plus salt? How about paint plus crayons? Paint plus starch? Glue? Soap? Try all the combinations on the next six pages for some super-special paintings.

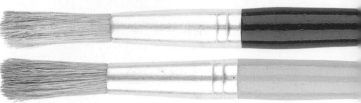

Black acrylic and colored tempera paints

Paintbrushes

Materials needed:

Dish

Glitter

Salt

Crayons

Paper

Glue

Watercolor paints and water

This wet-on-wet painting looks like a flower.

Here's a finished salt painting.

Wet on Wet

1 Dip your brush in clean water and wet your whole paper. Then wet one pad of watercolor paint and load the brush. Brush the wet color onto the wet paper.

2 Try making dots and lines. Watch the color explode! Rinse your brush and add a second color. See how the two colors blend.

Salt

Try shaking salt on one of your paintings while it's still wet. Let it dry and then brush off the salt. It will make designs in the paint.

Paint Plus . . .

. . . Crayons. Use crayons to make rubbings of interesting textures around your house. Then paint over them with watercolors.

. . . Marker. Make a wet-on-wet painting as shown in steps 1 and 2 on page 211. (The colors in this painting look like a sunset.) Draw a scene on top of the painting when it's dry. This black drawing was done with a marker. A black drawing like this is called a *silhouette*.

. . . Starch and salt. Here's a finished painting done with paint, liquid starch and salt.

1 Mix ½ cup liquid starch, ⅛ cup water, and ½ cup of salt.

2 Divide the mixture into several dishes. Add 1 to 2 tablespoons of tempera paint to each dish and stir it up.

3 Use the mixture to make a bumpy painting. Let the texture and the colors inspire you to paint something from your imagination.

Paint Plus Glue

Here's a finished paint-plus-glue house.

Helpful Hints

- It's hard to draw details with glue in a plastic bag, so the larger the shapes are in your picture, the better.
- If you can, keep an old glue bottle, wash it out with warm soapy water, and fill it with the black glue. It will be easier to draw with! You can also buy black glue at some craft stores.

1 Make a pencil drawing on paper. Mix 1 teaspoon of black acrylic paint with 3 teaspoons of white glue. Stir it.

2 Spoon the black glue into a plastic bag. Snip a tiny hole in one corner. Squeeze the glue along your drawing. Let it dry.

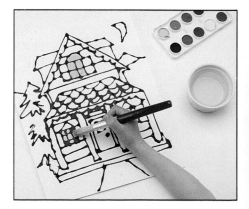

3 Use watercolor paints to color in the shapes you outlined with the black glue.

This alien puppet is painted with tempera paint on lightweight, black cardboard. To make him sparkle, wait for the paint to dry, then draw lines with white glue and sprinkle glitter on the wet glue. He'd look great at night with a flashlight shining on him!

This movie-star puppet has shiny sunglasses, dress and shoes. You can get the same shiny results by mixing tempera paint with a few drops of white glue, then brushing on those areas. Sprinkle on colored glitter while the gluey paint is still wet. The glue in the paint helps the glitter stick to it.

Paint Plus Soap

Here's a lumpy camel made with paint mixed with soap!

1 Mix 1½ cups of laundry soap flakes with 1 cup of warm water. Beat it with an electric mixer until it's stiff.

2 Divide the soap mixture into several bowls. Add food coloring or paint to each bowl and stir.

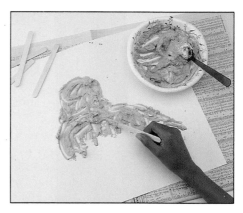

3 Use your fingers or craft sticks to spread the thick paint on cardboard or heavy paper.